My Kind of Sad

What It's Like to Be Young and Depressed

My Kind of Sad

What It's Like to Be Young and Depressed

Kate Scowen

Art by Jeff Szuc

Annick Press
Toronto • New York • Vancouver

This book contains general reference information about depression in youth. It is not intended as a substitute for the advice of a trained medical professional. Readers should not attempt to diagnose or treat themselves or their children based on the material contained in this book, but rather should consult an appropriate medical or psychiatric professional before starting or stopping any medication and before implementing any other therapy discussed in this book. The authors and publisher are not responsible for any adverse effects resulting from the information contained in this book.

©2006 Kate Scowen (text)
with editorial input from Allen Flaming
©2006 Jeff Szuc (cover and interior art)
Cover and interior design by Sheryl Shapiro
Cover image: istockphoto Inc./Eva Serrabassa

Annick Press Ltd.

We acknowledge the support of the Canada Council for the Arts, the Ontario Arts Council, and the Government of Canada through the Book Publishing Industry Development Program (BPIDP) for our publishing activities.

Cataloging in Publication

Scowen, Kate
        My kind of sad : what it's like to be young and depressed /
Kate Scowen ; art by Jeff Szuc.

Includes bibliographical references and index.
ISBN-13: 978-1-55037-941-9 (bound)
ISBN-10: 1-55037-941-0 (bound)
ISBN-13: 978-1-55037-940-2 (pbk.)
ISBN-10: 1-55037-940-2 (pbk.)

        1. Depression, Mental—Juvenile literature.   2. Depression in adolescence—Popular works.   I. Szuc, Jeff II. Title.

RC537.S38 2006   j616.85'27   C2005-906896-5

The text was typeset in ACaslon and Preface.

Distributed in Canada by: Published in the U.S.A. by Annick Press (U.S.) Ltd.
Firefly Books Ltd.   Distributed in the U.S.A. by:
66 Leek Crescent   Firefly Books (U.S.) Inc.
Richmond Hill, ON   P.O. Box 1338
L4B 1H1   Ellicott Station
                                   Buffalo, NY 14205

Printed and bound in Canada by Friesens, Altona, Manitoba
Visit us at: www.annickpress.com

Contents

Acknowledgments

This book is a reflection of the many youth and parents who took the time to meet with me and speak about their experiences with adolescence, moodiness, and depression. I would like to thank all of them—without their stories this book would seem empty. I would also like to thank the many youth workers, doctors, and therapists who connected me with youth and who facilitated the interview process.

While there are so many who offered advice, support, and insight, two people in particular require special mention here. Dr. Marshall Korenblum, Chief Psychiatrist at Hincks-Dellcrest Centre for Children in Toronto, provided professional guidance that ensured clinical accuracy and sensitivity. He also contributed to the text in the treatment section (chapter 10) and produced the afterword, which offers practical information and links to resources. Allen Flaming offered his friendship and support throughout the conception, researching, and writing of this book. His editorial and professional input helped to make sense of an overwhelming amount of information. Many thanks to both of you.

For Sydney, Hatley, and Quinn
        —K.S.

INTRODUCTION

This book is about a lot more than depression. It's about being an adolescent and how that shapes you. It's about what happens when your moods and habits move beyond the everyday and become harmful. And it's about how to recognize that and know when to get some help.

We all get moody sometimes. Our moods can fluctuate throughout the day without much warning. Depending on what is happening in our lives, our moods can be more visible sometimes than at other times. It's all part of being human. Imagine a world without moods or emotions—no laughing at funny jokes, no crying when your feelings are hurt, no anger when someone pushes you, no fear watching a scary movie—what a boring world that would be.

When you're little, chances are your emotions and moods are managed by your parents. If you fall and hurt yourself, they pick you up and brush you off. If someone hurts your feelings, they mediate the conflict for you and help to restart your friendship. As an adolescent, this begins to change. Not only do you *want* your parents to be less involved, they just aren't around as much. You're probably spending more time at school and more time with your friends. This all happens at a time when you are going through some major physical and emotional changes.

Your brain and your body are both changing in weird and wonderful ways. Now you have to figure out how to navigate the world on your own at a time when you're experiencing some serious inner chaos. This can be stressful and can certainly affect your moods. In this way, moodiness is a normal part of adolescence. The relationship between your moods, the world around you, and your life as an adolescent is explored in Part I.

Depression is more than moodiness; it is a mood disorder. A mood disorder is different from moodiness in that it is not a phase or something that will necessarily pass on its own. Depression may have one specific clinical description, but it's really so many different things. We get a real glimpse of this through the personal stories of youth who generously contributed to this book. Moodiness, depression, anxiety, mania, eating disorders, self-harming, substance abuse, and suicide are some of the issues that came up in their stories. These issues and their connection with adolescent depression are presented in Part II.

A friend may be able to cheer you up when you're feeling sad, but if you are clinically depressed or struggling with another mood disorder, you need to get some professional help. That help can come in a variety of forms, and you may need to spend some time finding out what suits you best. Different kinds of therapies and treatments are discussed in Part III.

This book is not going to give you a quick fix for depression or some magic formula for getting through adolescence. There is none. What this book *will* do is tell you what depression is and how it is different from being sad. I hope it will make you think a bit about what it means to be an adolescent. It will suggest ways to get help and will provide you with resources where you can find that help. If you are a friend of someone who you think is depressed or is struggling with some of the other issues explored in this book, it will give you some ideas on how you might be able to help.

A GUIDE TO READING THIS BOOK

Depression is an illness that has afflicted humankind since the earliest times. People have studied it, written about it, sung about it, and painted it. There are an incredible number of resources on depression out there, but few of them are geared specifically to youth. This is because adolescent depression has only been recognized as a medical diagnosis in the past 25 years. Today's climbing rates of adolescent depression have parents, sociologists, and medical professionals trying to figure out what is going on. Things are changing quickly, new treatments are being developed, and new discoveries about depression and adolescence are being made. The challenge in this book was to highlight the issues that might be important to you without boring you with clinical descriptions or overwhelming you with information.

If you are reading this book, you may fall into one of the following categories:

◆ You have been feeling kind of moody lately and are curious to find out if your moods are part of "normal" adolescence or something more.

◆ You have been diagnosed as having clinical depression or another mood disorder and want to find out more about what is going on with you.

◆ You have a friend or sibling who you think might be depressed and want to find out more about the issue so you can provide some help.

◆ Your parents bought it for you and suggested that you talk about it with them after you've finished reading it.

These are all good reasons to read this book (although the last one might be a little frightening!). There is no best way to read this book, as each person will get something different out of it. You may be interested in a specific issue and turn immediately to that chapter. You may start at the beginning but skip over chapters that you don't think mean anything to you right now. That's fine. I hope you are able to take from this book whatever it is you need. For some, this book may be as far as they want to go. For others, it may be the starting point from which they begin their journey, exploring the experience of being an adolescent and the many things that may affect their happiness. The more you know about yourself and how you fit into the world around you, the better equipped you will be to tackle the many challenges of life.

At the end of the book there is a section called **CHECK IT OUT**. This contains information on resources that you might want to look into if you are interested in exploring a particular issue further. I have tried to choose resources that will be appropriate for adolescents, but, given the variety of your ages and experiences, this was a challenge. I have briefly described each listing, which I hope will make it easier for you to decide what might appeal to you. Please use your good judgment as to what is appropriate for you when exploring these resources. If you see this symbol in the book, that means you will find further information and resources in the Check It Out section.

In researching this book, I interviewed many youth and their family members about their experiences with depression and other related issues. The stories at the beginning of each chapter in Part II and many of the quotes throughout the book were drawn from these interviews. In order to protect their privacy, people's names have been changed. It is important to remember that, while their personal experiences may help you understand what it is like to be bipolar or to struggle with an eating disorder, everyone's experience will be different. There is no clear path through depression or other mood disorders; we each bring our own unique experiences, insights, and challenges into the picture. While you may relate to some of the ideas or struggles outlined in the stories, your personal experience will be just that—personal and unique. Your feelings, successes, and setbacks may be more or less intense, depending on your personal circumstances.

The afterword by Dr. Marshall Korenblum beginning on page 141 contains important information on how to figure out when you need help, and how and where you can get it. On page 144 you will find a list of resources that will link you to 24-hour hotlines you can call if you have a simple question, if you just need someone to talk to, or if you are in crisis.

WARNING

Some of the issues discussed in this book are intense. Please be aware that this book contains stories that may be upsetting for people dealing with issues such as cutting, suicide, and eating disorders. You know yourself best. If you feel you may not be able to handle it, wait. There's no rush—this book isn't going anywhere. You can even skip over a chapter that you think you might not be able to handle right now. When you feel you're ready to read it, make sure you have a dialogue going with someone who can support you—a counselor, an adult, a friend. Let this person know what you are up to and where you are at so they can look out for you. Reading about other people's experiences can be really helpful, but it can also bring back lots of memories of your own experiences, good and bad. Make sure you have all the support you need so you can get the most out of this book.

Part I:
The Background

Chapter 1
Depression: Then and Now

The world you live in and your personal experiences of it are going to have a tremendous impact on your mood and your outlook on life. The world we live in today is changing at an incredible pace. This chapter explores depression within the context of our world, both historically and in the "here and now." Understanding what is going on around you and how it might affect you can help you to better understand yourself. Once you've done that, you can tackle your moods and even your depression with more confidence.

DEPRESSION THROUGH THE AGES

Depression has plagued humankind since the beginning of time. The word *depression* comes from the Latin terms *de* (down from) and *premere* (to press)—meaning "to be pressed down." Some other early terms used to describe feelings of sadness and of being "pressed down" include *dejection*, *melancholia*, and *depression of spirits*.

Throughout history, there has been much confusion as to whether depression itself was a disease or whether it was a combination of the signs and symptoms of another disease. While thinking varied across the globe, treatments and therapeutic approaches in the ancient world were often cruel, unreasonable, and downright silly.

CHECK

IT OUT

page 146

During Hippocratic times (early fifth century BCE), it was believed that people's bodies were balanced by four elements (humors): blood, yellow bile, phlegm, and black bile. An excess of black bile in the body was blamed for many illnesses, including headaches, epilepsy, vertigo, spasms, and a depression of spirits. Too much black bile was thought to affect the brain, which Hippocrates identified as the center of emotion and mental illness (not unlike our thinking today). Hippocrates was the first to treat depression with oral remedies and an early form of talk therapy.

In the Middle Ages (from the late 5th to the 15th century CE), many people thought depression was the result of an imperfect soul, and that it was punishment for having angered God or for having sinned. During the Inquisition, some people were fined or imprisoned for their depression. People also believed that those who suffered from mental illness were possessed by devils and demons. People suffering from depression were sent to work in manual labor camps, and their families and friends were told to abandon them. The hope was that work and isolation would redeem them and that God would forgive them.

During the Renaissance (16th and 17th centuries), depression was linked to two pressing social issues: genius and witchcraft. The English romanticized depression (then called melancholia) as a kind of soulfulness and a sign of genius. It was considered an illness that was beyond the control of those suffering from it, and treatments included exercise, listening to music, and changes in diet. The Dutch retained the earlier thinking that depression was caused by some sort of evil possession, although they did believe that it was not the fault of the depressed person. Exorcisms were often attempted to deliver evil spirits from the bodies of the possessed. During this time, some argued that witches were not really evil, just foolish and depressed old women. The idea that these women were mentally ill saved many of them from being executed.

The Age of Reason (18th century) was probably the worst time to be depressed. At this point in history, people's thinking turned from the soulful to the scientific. The human body was regarded as a machine, a scientific wonder, and someone who was depressed was considered to have no self-discipline. Severe punishments were imposed on the depressed and mentally ill. They were sentenced to live in asylums as social outcasts, without rights and with no chance of recovery. For this reason, those who were not severely mentally ill kept their depression hidden and suffered alone.

IN THE 18TH CENTURY

YOU HID YOUR DEPRESSION AND SUFFERED ALONE.

Things got a bit better in the Romantic and Victorian eras (19th century), as those who suffered from melancholia were considered once again to be brilliant and soulful. During this time, the depressed were treated as people, not as animals or moral deviants. Many new asylums were opened that focused on treating the individual, and these became a sort of community for those who lived in them. Families willingly admitted their loved ones into the asylums, no longer fearing they might be mistreated. Treatments for depression included walks, reading, music, and exercise. At this time people also reverted to the fifth-century belief that depression was a disease of the brain, and brain autopsies became quite common, especially when someone committed suicide.

In modern times (20th century) there have been two schools of thought about depression and mental illness. Sigmund Freud talked about the power of the mind's subconscious, and proposed the important idea that depression is really anger turned inwards. Emil Kraepelin proposed that depression is biochemical and has strong links to heredity, implying that if you are genetically predisposed to depression, then you are pretty much doomed. A man named Adolf Meyer bridged these two theories, proposing that each person is unique and capable of change. He believed that people's social environment has a great impact on how they feel and who they are. In 1950 the first antidepressant was developed, which led the way to many new treatments for depression and other mental illnesses.

FREUD
1856 – 1939

EVERY GENERATION HAS ITS CHALLENGES

Adolescence is a time of real and important changes, and by all means it is one of the most challenging times in a person's life.

"The children now love luxury; they have bad manners, contempt for authority; they show disrespect for elders and love chatter in place of exercise. Children are now tyrants, not the servants of their households. They no longer rise when elders enter the room. They contradict their parents, chatter before company, gobble up dainties at the table, cross their legs, and tyrannize their teachers."
— Socrates

Whatever is happening in the world around you when you are going through adolescence will make an impression on you. It will affect your family and how they interact with you, it will affect your community and how they can support you, and it will affect your friends and how they balance you.

Every generation likes to make its claim to having it especially hard. In the 1930s it was the Great Depression, in the 1940s it was World War II, in the 1950s it was conservatism, in the 1960s it was the sexual revolution, in the 1970s it was the Cold War, in the 1980s it was corporate dominance, and in the 1990s it was the breakdown of the traditional family structure. There are broad cultural and social influences

1930s...   1950s...   1960s...   1980s...   2000+

within each generation that impact the members of that generation and how they perceive the world.

"Adolescence is the period during which a young person learns who he is, and what he really feels. It is the time during which he differentiates himself from his culture, though on the culture's terms."
— Edgar Friedenberg, *The Vanishing Adolescent*

So, it may have been hard to be an adolescent in the 1930s because your family may have had to struggle to make ends meet. Perhaps you had to get a job at an early age and leave school to help out. Being an adolescent in the 1990s would have been equally challenging, because maybe your family had fallen apart. Perhaps you were shuffled back and forth between caregivers, isolated from a sense of family belonging, and caught in the middle of your parents' battles with each other.

However, that same adolescent who grew up in the Depression may have become an extremely successful business person later in life, thanks to an early exposure to hard work and a strong sense of financial responsibility. Similarly, the adolescent of the nineties may have grown up with an eagerness to explore and try new things, leading to a fulfilling life of adventure and success, thanks to an early sense of independence and an ability to adapt to change. Blessing or curse, whatever you're living through shapes who you are.

Brave New World

The current generation of adolescents have grown up at a time of great insecurity worldwide. The new millennium was anxiously anticipated around the world, mostly with fear and trepidation. Remember the Y2K panic? Would all computers crash, bringing the world to a grinding halt, as the clock struck twelve on January 1, 2000? Well, despite our global ability to prepare for, talk about, imagine, and predict the worst, nothing happened. But if you were, let's say, 10 in 2000, you would surely have felt the anxiety and pressure the rest of the world was feeling about moving into a new millennium. By the age of 10 we become increasingly aware of the world around us and can understand more and more of the adult conversations buzzing in our ears. So this may have been your first introduction to the instability of the world around you—a fairly frightening initiation into adolescence. Since then, countless issues and crises have arisen, which will undoubtedly have added to the stress of the end of your childhood: September 11, the war in Iraq, SARS, mad cow disease, and tsunamis, to name a few.

"The remarkable thing about television is that it permits several million people to laugh at the same joke and still feel lonely."
— T.S. Eliot

The reason we know so much about all of this stuff is that we live in such a global world. Everything is televised and everything is talked about. How many times did we need to see the planes flying into the World Trade Center? To be bombarded relentlessly by images of all of these horrific events and issues is stressful. Terrorism, war, and disease make us all feel vulnerable. These used to be adult worries; now they are part of everyone's psyche. They are not necessarily more serious than the worries of the past, but thanks to the media they are our ever-present reality, our "new normal." Deciding which generation had it harder is not going to make anything easier. Understanding the challenges of your youth might.

NEW RESEARCH INTO THE BRAIN

Many adults who suffer from depression report that their first depressive episode occurred in adolescence. It wasn't until about 1980 that doctors believed adolescents could actually suffer from depression. Before that time, they didn't think that adolescents were mature enough to experience depression. Now, adolescent depression is something everybody knows about. Media reports highlight new research and discoveries on an almost weekly basis, making it hard to know what is really going on. What we do know is that in the United States approximately 3.5 million children and teenagers suffer from depression. While we used to assume that moodiness and antisocial behavior were normal passages of adolescence, we now know differently.

"Twenty percent—one in five—of teenagers report that they have had a major depressive episode that went untreated during their adolescence."
— Harold Koplewicz, *More Than Moody*

There is some debate about the increase in adolescent depression. Some people believe that it has always been there, but that there is better identification and reporting of it today. Others claim that the fast-paced changes in our global world are increasing stress levels in adolescents, triggering depression. Whatever the cause, adolescent depression poses some interesting challenges for the scientific world.

New Discoveries

In the past, scientists and doctors learned about mental health disorders in part by studying the brains of dead people. They cut them open, looked inside them, and identified ways in which a healthy brain was different from an unhealthy one. Given that a lot of the cadavers they worked on were adult, they knew little about the brain development and patterns of adolescents. There are now machines and tools that make looking into your brain (while you're still alive) a lot easier. MRIs (magnetic resonance imaging machines) make easy work of brain scans, and studies are being done that track the brain development of adolescents. What's being discovered is interesting.

It was once believed that your brain was fully developed by the age of 12, when it is fully grown in size. It turns out that your brain continues to change until around the age of 25. These changes take place inside your full-grown brain and have to do with brain cell connections and wiring. In fact, your brain undergoes two major periods of internal growth: in utero (while you are floating around in your mother's belly) and in adolescence. During adolescence, your brain starts pruning itself (cutting connections) and proliferating (making new connections) as it becomes more efficient. This important stage in your brain development leads you into adulthood, as your brain prepares itself to perform its highest mental functions. So, while you may feel old enough and responsible enough to be treated like an adult, the fact is your brain is not quite there yet.

DURING ADOLESCENCE YOUR BRAIN **REWIRES** ITSELF FOR **EFFICIENCY**.

The direction in which the brain matures has a major effect on your readiness for the adult world. The maturing starts at the back of the brain and slowly moves to the front. At the back of your brain is the cerebellum, which affects physical coordination and supports higher learning (such as math and languages). This is the first part of your brain to be affected by the wave of pruning and proliferation in adolescence, and it keeps on changing and growing until you are in your early 20s.

The last part of your brain to mature may actually be the most important (and may be what is keeping you from convincing your parents that you are ready for more independence). As your brain development slowly moves forward, it finally reaches your prefrontal cortex, the part of your brain that enables you to make rational decisions. So, by the time you are about 25, your brain has finished most of its growing, pruning, and proliferation, and you are ready to enter the realm of adulthood armed with your most important asset: a fully matured brain.

CHECK IT OUT
page 146

New research has shed light on the role of your brain chemistry (how your brain works) in two important issues: adolescent behavior and adolescent depression. Adolescent moodiness and irrational behavior may not be the result of hormones alone—your mutating brain may also be to blame. It seems probable too that abnormalities in the pruning process during adolescence may lead to or unmask mental health issues, such as depression, schizophrenia, or bipolar disorder.

New Treatments

A lot of progress has been made in improving drug therapies for adults suffering from depression and other mood disorders. Again, because adolescent depression is a newly identified issue, drug therapy is fairly controversial.

"Among American children under 18, antidepressant use rose 49 percent in just four years, from 1998 to 2002." — Paul Raeburn, *Psychology Today*

You probably know someone who is on an antidepressant, or at least you have heard of someone in your school or community who is. Prozac, Zoloft, Paxil—these have almost become household names. North American culture seems to want quick fixes to its problems, and in many ways antidepressants are the perfect answer. Antidepressants are medications that alter your brain chemistry and balance your moods. As North American adults try to juggle their hectic schedules, there is little time left to figure out what is wrong with their children. Just as TV makes a great babysitter, antidepressants make a great stabilizer. This may be a cynical view, but it is not uncommon. Fears that we may be medicating the personalities and individuality out of our children are present. These fears may be valid in some cases, but for **page 147** many children and their families antidepressants are a necessity. While we don't want to medicate the moodiness out of adolescence, controlling the rages and mania of bipolar disorder or the depths of despair of clinical depression can often only be done with antidepressants.

A COMBINATION OF MEDICATION & TALKING

While there has been a fair bit of research done on the benefits and impacts of antidepressant use in adults, no one really knows what long-term effects the extended use of certain drugs will have on an adolescent brain that is still developing. One study has indicated that antidepressants are actually ineffective when used by adolescents. Other studies have demonstrated that adolescents taking antidepressants may be at an increased risk of suicidal thoughts and behavior. This is not to say that drug therapy does not work or should not be used in adolescents—in many cases it is a life-saver—but it needs to be managed and monitored carefully. In fact, recent reports have indicated that the most effective treatment for adolescents struggling with depression is a combination of medication and talk therapy. For more information on medications and treatments, see chapter 10.

LITTLE BLACK BOXES ◀ • • • • • • • • • • • • • • •

In October 2004, the U.S. Food and Drug Administration announced that manufacturers of all antidepressant drugs must include in their labeling a boxed warning about the increased risk of suicidality (suicidal thinking and behavior) in children and adolescents being treated with these medications. This action was taken in response to the results of 24 controlled clinical studies on 9 antidepressants. These studies revealed that in the first few months of treatment, children and adolescents whose depression was treated with antidepressants were more likely to experience suicidal thoughts and behavior than those treated with a placebo.

GOOD NEWS

What's good about all of this research is that we are now able to recognize and treat adolescent depression much faster and more efficiently than before. As a society, we are more and more willing to talk about what ails us, and depression, as well as many other mental health disorders, has become more accepted.

"I definitely think, though, when I was depressed, I felt like I was weird, I was a weirdo, people would think I was crazy and stuff. But now I think, when people are depressed, it's, like, okay. Everybody knows so much about depression. It's something people have started talking about a lot." Claire, 17

STARS LIKE US

There is no shortage of celebrities who are willing to come forward and tell us about their struggles with depression and related issues. In many ways this is a good thing, as it helps to bring these issues to the public's attention and sort of "normalizes" them.

Writers, poets, actors, painters, and musicians have struggled with these issues for centuries. Some suggest that there is a link between the creative process and depression and mania. Here are some people you may have heard of who struggled with depression and other mood disorders.

page 147

CHECK IT OUT

Charles Schulz (*Peanuts* cartoonist)
Diana, Princess of Wales
Eugene O'Neill (author)
Jackson Pollock (painter)
John Lennon (musician)
Kurt Cobain (musician)
Kurt Vonnegut (author)
Ludwig von Beethoven (composer)
Mark Twain (author)
Marilyn Monroe (actress)
Michelangelo Buonarroti (painter, sculptor)
Nick Drake (musician)
Sylvia Plath (author)
Vincent Van Gogh (painter)
Virginia Woolf (author)
Vivien Leigh (actress)
Winston Churchill (politician)

Chapter 2
Adolescence: Identity and Chaos

There are a lot of things in your life that will affect you as you pass through adolescence into adulthood. This is probably the most chaotic period of your life, so it is no great wonder that you may feel sad at times. This chapter looks at the many issues that can affect your moods as an adolescent. It also takes a peek at some of the important things that can shift your moodiness from sadness to real depression.

"I think that one of the things that's really hard about adolescence is that, to a certain extent, it's a period of severe disillusionment."
Mary, 21

Adolescence, by definition, is the age between the start of puberty and adulthood. For some of you, puberty may start at the age of 10, while for others it may begin much later. Even if you're not going through puberty by the age of 12, you are still an adolescent, or at least you are working up to it; your friends and social structure are all geared towards keeping you within that time frame. The most important thing that's happening to you now is that you are developing your personal identity, figuring out who you are and what your place is in the world.

"... if the function of adolescence is self-definition, one would expect it to be very difficult in a society which suffers from a dearth of individuality and in which alienation is a crucial problem."
— Edgar Friedenberg, *The Vanishing Adolescent*

You've made it through childhood and you've tackled some important things: friendships and school, primarily. Now, your main influence and focus becomes your friends, as you start to break away from your family a bit. You have more freedom to come and go as you please, and you also have more responsibility to make sure you get your schoolwork done, to come home on time, and to be basically pleasant to the people around you.

BRAINS, HORMONES, AND PERSONALITY

"Especially in this grade [grade 9] I notice some of my friends, even me, we're just complete mood freaks. One minute we're all happy, the next we're like, 'Oh! Go away!'" Alice, 15

At this time of your life, you are going through huge emotional and physical changes. Your body is morphing into something slightly unfamiliar, and your moods can seem un-controllable. You don't want to be mean, but everyone around you is just so irri-  tating. Your body changes are pretty straightforward, and there are many resources that will explain this to you with humor and sensitivity. The emotional changes are something else altogether.

page 148

CHECK IT OUT

Although your brain is a part of your body, as you go through adolescence it seems to take on a life of its own. As discussed in the previous chapter, your adolescent brain shapes itself as it builds and prunes connections. Increasing rates of adolescent depression and the fact that many other mental health disorders, such as schizophrenia, unfold in adolescence have led scientists to believe that there is a connection between the hormones released during adolescence and brain chemistry. The sex hormones that come rushing through you as a teenager, turning your body into the adult version of itself, can affect your brain chemistry by influencing the pruning process. It is also believed that a stressful life event (such as a divorce, death, or violence) can alter your brain chemistry, affecting the pruning process and triggering depression and other mental health issues.

SEROTONIN AND MOOD

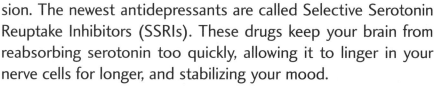

Serotonin is a compound that occurs naturally in your brain and is released from one nerve cell to another. It is then reabsorbed back into the first nerve cell and sent out again. If too much is reabsorbed by the first nerve cell, not enough is sent back out, and the result is an imbalance of serotonin in your brain. Low levels of serotonin have been found in people who suffer from depression. The newest antidepressants are called Selective Serotonin Reuptake Inhibitors (SSRIs). These drugs keep your brain from reabsorbing serotonin too quickly, allowing it to linger in your nerve cells for longer, and stabilizing your mood.

Many adults still view hormones as slightly evil and mischievous little characters that float through your body and make you do all sorts of silly and irrational things: skip school, act goofy around someone you're attracted to, forget to call home when you promised, leave your room looking like a pigsty. In part they're right—it *is* hormones, but those hormones are sending wild messages to your brain, which is in turn making you do and feel some interesting (and important) things. So, while we once blamed adolescent chaos on hormones, we didn't really have a clear understanding of their power. Now we know that these hormones have a serious and long-term impact on your brain chemistry and development, and that these changes can affect your moods and behavior.

Forgetfulness and poor decision making may result from your chaotic brain, but let's not forget the role played by personality. Each of us has a unique personality, which will affect how we look at life and how we handle situations. Some of us are outgoing, some of us are willing to take risks, some of us are pessimistic—it's in our nature. Our personalities affect how we handle stress. Someone who learns as a child (with the support of parents or other caregivers) how to stay calm under pressure or how to negotiate a difficult situation is likely to be more resilient in adolescence. This resilience, which is actually a combination of your personality, your genes, and your life experiences, may protect you from depression.

"Sometimes I'll ask adults if they would ever go back to being 14 or whatever the age is we happen to be talking about, and without any kind of hesitation they all say, "No way!" and then they continue with reciting every detail of that year—who they had a crush on that didn't like them back, the white skirt they had on when they got their period in the middle of math. We are constantly reminded that the teenage years are just plain old tough, and I think that's why it's so hard to decide if you're depressed or just blue." Susan, 19

SEXUALITY

As you go through puberty and your body starts to change, your sexual interest in other people begins to develop. Some people go through this earlier than others, but it happens to all of us. For many of us, this is when we figure out if we are attracted to the opposite sex or the same sex. Although North American society has gone through some major transformations regarding same-sex relationships, there is still a lot of bias and negativity where homosexuality is concerned. Figuring out if you are straight, gay, or bisexual can be tough. You may have the support of your friends when you come out, but telling your family might never be an option. Your parents' and/or other family members' cultural or religious beliefs may conflict with your sexuality or other lifestyle choices. This can present some significant barriers to your happiness.

CHECK IT OUT
page 148

And then there's the whole dating thing. Going out on a date or even mustering up the courage to ask someone out can be incredibly stressful (one of those things that doesn't necessarily get easier with age). A first breakup can be devastating, making you question your whole being—especially if you are the one who gets dumped. Why don't they like me? Aren't I good/ funny/attractive enough? Usually, after experiencing your first rejection, you realize that you will survive, and although it really hurts, you may learn a bit about yourself. So, even though rejection is always hard, the first one, which usually takes place in adolescence, is extra harsh—you don't have the cushion of experience to soften the blow.

page 148

Dating and sexuality open the door to a host of other potentially mood-defining moments. Pregnancy, rape, and STIs (sexually transmitted infections) can all be part of the package. This is serious stuff to have to negotiate, and even more difficult when you are still figuring out who you are and what you want.

page 148

Another issue that can get very complicated is physical and/or emotional abuse within a relationship. Some people find themselves hooked up with someone who puts them down, pushes them around, or gets really jealous when they pay attention to others. These controlling behaviors can be really damaging (emotionally and physically) to the person who is being abused. If you find that you're in this kind of relationship, or if you know someone who is, you need to get help.

page 148

Who Likes Who?

It seems that kids are getting into sex at a much earlier age than their parents' generation did. Media stories of girls giving blow jobs to their boyfriends in the schoolyard and reported rates of teen pregnancy throw parents into nervous fits of delirium. Some people relate this behavior to low self-esteem and peer pressure. Some say it's a response to media images that confuse youth about what is appropriate. We are such a society of mixed messages that it's hard to get it straight. Regardless of your influence, you will have to make these first important decisions on your own. Parents try to guide you, but at an age when their influence is being replaced by that of your friends, it may be confusing trying to figure out whom you should listen to. Just remember that you know yourself best, and you shouldn't do anything that you don't want to do or that makes you uncomfortable. The most important person to listen to is yourself.

FAMILIES

"I think it's really confusing for kids when they see the adults around them saying one thing about being the parent and taking care of them, then not actually being prepared to take care of them. So I think sometimes kids get into problems because adults don't make the sacrifices they have to make." Jane, parent

In the past 20 years, the definition of family has changed dramatically. The idea of a married couple staying that way, raising four kids while the father goes out to work and the

mother stays home, is long gone. One thing that hasn't changed is the complicated nature of family relationships. Some parents are in conflict, some siblings can't stand each other, some families stay together when perhaps it would be better if they didn't, some never

were together. Whatever your family picture looks like, it has a great influence on you as you go through adolescence, and it can add to your stress and moodiness.

If your family is not the cause of your depression, it can be an incredible support system for you. Your family is often made up of the people who know and love you the best, and their happiness is connected to yours. Even if they are really irritating at certain points in your life (and they most probably will be), try not to alienate yourself from them. When it comes to a crisis, it's amazing how families can pull together and fight for each other. And even if you don't connect with your immediate family, there may be an aunt, cousin, or in-law who gets your point of view and cares about where you are headed.

FRIENDS

During adolescence your friends become the foundation of your life. Parents worry endlessly that you might not be hanging out with the right crowd as their influence is replaced by that of your friends—in their minds, the wrong crowd could lead you down the path to delinquency. For the most part, kids make the right choices.

CHECK IT OUT

page 149

"Don't worry about making new friends, because there are others worrying the same thing. In all the people coming to school, there's bound to be somebody who likes you." Alice, 15

Finding a group to fit into can be hard. Groups of friends act like a sort of family. It is a place where you belong, where you will be protected from the overwhelming sea of kids out there. There are usually one or two leaders in the group, who act as a kind of magnet, drawing other members to them. They set the

FINDING A GROUP TO FIT INTO CAN BE REALLY HARD.

tone for the group and can influence other members' interests. Often kids will be drawn to groups that share similar interests (sports, drama, computers), but sometimes kids will look for acceptance in a group just to gain popularity.

"Well, there are the preppy ones, but they aren't extreme. You can see the difference between all of them. There are the hard-core punks that are all together. Then there are the people that aren't really punks and aren't really preppy, they're just in the middle, so there's that little group which usually chains off into other little groups. Then there's the extreme preps." Alice, 15

GROUPS ARE OFTEN FORMED AROUND SIMILAR INTERESTS.

Friendships and popularity can be based on good looks and "good things." In some groups you're desirable if you have the right cell phone, clothes, and shoes. In others, your taste in music or your computer skills may secure your position. Kids can be socially tormented and isolated for not having what it takes to fit in. Even though this kind of selection may begin in kindergarten, it seems to hit its peak in adolescence. So, just when you're feeling your most vulnerable, the playing field gets bigger and the rules begin to change.

Bullying is an issue that everyone knows about but not everyone experiences. Being bullied means more than being pushed around; it can mean name calling, leaving someone out of a group (exclusion), harassment, racism, and threatening. People who are being bullied at school or in their community often feel isolated, not wanted, and unsafe. This kind of torment and fear can definitely affect how people perceive themselves

and their place in the world. Believe it or not, bullies themselves can also feel lousy. The anger and frustration that leads to bullying can be caused by depression or other stressful life situations. This doesn't mean bullying is acceptable, but sometimes it helps to consider where the bully is coming from. Why are bullies so angry, and why do they feel a need to push other kids around?

CHECK IT OUT

page 149

SCHOOL

The influence of school is huge. It's where it all happens for you (unless, of course, you are home-schooled or you have "opted out" of school for a while). It's learning and socializing all in one. The pressure can be unbelievable. The politics, the social hierarchy, the academic pressure—these are all the things that make or break us in adolescence. A bad day at school can put you in a mood that sets your tone for the rest of the day. By the time you get home, you just want to be alone, but the demands may not end. You still have homework, chores, and a responsibility to be pleasant to your family. That can be hard.

"In grade 7, I was starting at a new school, having to make new friends, and having to do this and that. Leaving grade 6 and your friends that you've known since kindergarten, being scared of growing up and having things change, really caught me." Claire, 17

School can be particularly difficult because it is something most adolescents cannot escape. If an adult is unhappy at work or is having a conflict with someone in the community, they have the opportunity to start over again somewhere new; they can change jobs or move away. As an adolescent, you are more likely to be bound by the academic and social limits of your school. If things are not going well there, your whole world can seem overwhelming.

"It would mostly be me worrying about what was going to happen and what the other people would think because I hadn't been there [at school] for a while. Depression isn't visible. It's not like I broke my leg and they could see the cast and know why I'd been off. Teenagers talk about stuff, so who knew what the rumors were. I don't really care. I say I don't care what people think, but then it's like, 'They're all looking at me. Oh my God!' But I had this constant pain in my chest when I went to school. It was this burning sensation that would go from my chest up into my throat. It was strange."
Caroline, 19

Another major issue around school is the enormous pressure to do well academically. Worries about getting good grades so you will get into the right college and secure your future can start as early as grade 7. This kind of pressure can make the future seem really scary and out of control for the best student. If you struggle at school, you may feel as if your future is already doomed to failure.

"It was scary because my friends knew they were going to college and they even knew what they wanted to do when they graduated. When they asked me, I was like, 'I don't know. I'm thinking about going here, but I'm not really sure what I want to be when I grow up.' I'm not even sure what I'm going to do after high school." Victor, 18

It's important to know that many schools offer programs that are flexible (part-time courses) and that can meet the needs of someone who might want to take a break. There are also options such as summer school or correspondence school, which can help keep you on track if you have to take some time off. Your school guidance counselor or teacher should be able to help you find out what is available to you.

LIFE CIRCUMSTANCES

Everyone's story is different. You can be rich, poor, healthy, sick—whatever. You each have your own story. It's that story that shapes who you are. It shapes who you are because it influences what you see and do in life. If you grow up in poverty, you might live in a neighborhood where crime and drug use are in your face, all the time. On your daily walk to school you may get to know people who are down on their luck, living on the street, and doing extraordinary things just to survive. If you are living in a middle-class suburb, chances are the scenery on your daily walk (or drive) to school is a bit different.

URBAN JUNGLE...

SUBURBIA...

► POVERTY AND DEPRESSION

Although depression does not discriminate—it can afflict anyone, rich or poor—in North America the rates of clinical depression are highest among people living in poverty. Someone who is living in poverty is more likely to experience the things that can trigger depression, such as a traumatic life event or financial stresses. In addition to this, people living in poverty may not have access to the supports that will help them to tackle their depression, such as proper medical care and medication, the distraction of jobs that get them out of the house every day, or supportive relationships that can help them recover.

If you have a serious childhood illness and spend a significant amount of time in hospitals and doctors' offices, you may be on your own a lot and be unable to join in after-school activities or sports teams. If you start life with a healthy body, you likely have the opportunity to try out for teams, play sports, and hang out with your friends regularly.

We don't get to choose these things; they just happen to us. It's never fair and it's not always easy, but this doesn't mean that you don't have any control over what is going on. You can make healthy choices and decisions that will affect you throughout your life. Besides, money and good fortune are no guarantee that you will be happy.

GENETICS

Some people face really difficult life circumstances as adolescents (abuse, poverty, poor health) and yet transform into adults who are confident, healthy, and happy. Other people, who have comparatively easy lives, become sidelined by mental health issues. No one really knows why this happens, but these variations in life circumstances lead many to believe that depression and other mental health issues are in part influenced by your genetics.

GENETIC RISK

The chance that you might get depression because you have a family history of it is called your "genetic risk" or "genetic predisposition." For example, if one of your parents has depression, you are more likely to suffer from it than someone whose parents do not have depression. If both of your parents are depressed, your risk of having depression is even greater. If you have a high genetic risk for depression, stressful life events could trigger depression in you, while the same events might not bother someone who is not genetically predisposed to depression.

There can even be genetic differences within the same family. So, you may suffer from depression but your brother may not, because he didn't inherit the same genes as you, even though his "genetic risk" was as high as yours.

Your best friend, whose parents got divorced after your friend's little brother became seriously ill, may be coping really well. On the other hand, you may become overwhelmed by depression when the person you like starts dating someone else. This is what can make depression so hard—it can take over your life without much warning, and sometimes with very little reason. Your seemingly smooth life may be turned upside down as your genetics unfold in adolescence.

It's important to remember that while statistics may explain your chances of developing a disease, they are not a life sentence. Many people whose parents or siblings struggle with mood disorders are not affected themselves.

CHECK IT OUT
page 150

IMAGES OF PERFECTION

Our genes can affect our happiness in other ways as well. In North America, we have a cultural obsession with beauty and self-improvement. The media and retail industries fuel a demand for endless makeover shows and magazines that teach us how to dress and style our hair, and for products that will make us look younger and sexier.

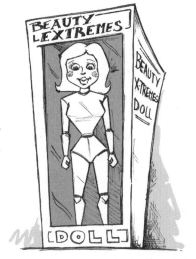

"People on TV always look good and it makes you want to look like them." Clifford, 18

Our physical features are determined in part by our genes. If you inherited your aunt's wide hips, your father's big nose, or your grandmother's skinny legs, that's just the luck of the draw. Unfortunately, the pressure to look like a movie star is greater than ever. It's hard enough being an adolescent at the best of times, but to grow up in a world that is obsessed with beauty is pretty hard to take, especially if you don't have the "natural resources" to play the game. Trying to keep up and fit in can lead some people to engage in unhealthy behaviors, such as excessive dieting. This can lead in turn to a much more complicated issue: eating disorders. For more information on eating disorders, see chapter 6.

CHECK IT OUT

page 150

MEDIA

We live in a world that is obsessed with media—television, videos, radio, movies, computers. They dominate our lives, and they bombard us with advertisements: pop-ups on our computers, commercials on TV, ads during the trailers before your movie. Your parents may get nostalgic about their relatively media-free childhoods, but let's face it, there's no turning back.

It has become almost a national pastime among adults to discuss how watching too much television is bad for children, and how watching violent movies and video games will make kids more violent. Parents also worry about the impact that the sexual content of music videos and television shows will have on adolescent sexual behavior. And they're not wrong to be worried. Research has proven the link between violence on television and youth crime. It has also been reported that adolescents who watch television shows with a lot of sexual content are likely to get into sexual activity earlier than those who do not.

What adults sometimes forget is that adolescents have a keen eye for hypocrisy. Adolescents know that although adults are expressing their concern about media content, it is adults who are producing this stuff and it is adults who are paying the cable bill, contributing to the growth of an industry that some claim is at the root of the downfall of today's youth.

It's important to remember that television is not real life. This may seem obvious, but with all of the reality TV shows out there, sometimes it's hard to tell the difference. Reality television is scripted, prompted, and edited in much the same way as your favorite sitcom. The illusion of reality is often just that—an illusion—and this can get confusing (for adults as much as adolescents). Television provides us with endless opportunities to be dissatisfied with what we have and who we are, as we compare ourselves to what we see on the screen. It's harder than ever to appreciate our real lives because we are being bombarded by unattainable and unrealistic images of happiness and perfection.

"I think part of the reason adolescents get depressed is because kids have become disconnected from reality. The media has created a new reality of human being. I think that's a big part of it, because people find it a lot harder to deal with a lot of things because they can't identify with themselves enough. There's too much 'artificial intelligence,' and it can only advance you to a certain point within yourself. You can't speak to a computer or a TV." Simon, 21

It's clear that kids are going to continue to watch television and movies and play video games. Whether you want to accept it or not, media does have an influence on you. In part, that's what it's there for—to shape your tastes, your spending, your opinions. It's a huge part of our culture, and unless you are prepared to never watch television again, you should at least try to look at it critically. There are a lot of media awareness and media literacy programs that will get you thinking about what is being thrown at you.

page 150

ANOTHER KIND OF SAD

"If you're just feeling down for a bit, it comes and goes. Depression lasts for an extended period, and you can't find the right thing to dig for." Simon, 21

All the things mentioned in this chapter can stress you out and affect your happiness and moods as an adolescent. Everyone gets bummed out or sad at some point. Usually, your friends and family will help to cheer you up, and within a few days you may begin to feel better. But a sadness that lasts a long time, over-whelms you, and seems to take over your life is another thing altogether. This is when you need to get some help—help that your friends and family may not be able to provide.

"Depression is so many things that it's difficult to just give it one definition. It shouldn't be confused with just having a few bad days in a row, or being unhappy for a couple of weeks due to some bad things occurring in your life. It's when you feel angry, or sad, or upset, or so many other things, nearly all the time. It's when you're not in control of the way you feel anymore, as if you just can't get a handle on things no matter how much you may want to or try." Susan, 19

Chapter 3
Depression: What Is It, Really?

If you have read through Part I of this book, you hopefully now have a better understanding of yourself, the world around you, and some of the critical factors that can contribute to your moodiness and depression. This chapter is going to explore what depression is and how you will know the difference between everyday adolescent moodiness and something much bigger—clinical depression.

When Caroline was 17, her family moved from the city to a small town. She had always been a quiet kid and this move was especially hard on her. In her first year at her new school she made a good friend, but suddenly that friend stopped talking to her, for no apparent reason. When Caroline asked her what was wrong, her friend would not talk about it. Instead, this friend started hanging out with Caroline's sister. Caroline felt deserted; her only friend had walked away from her. She was also facing a lot of pressure at school. Being in grade 11, she had to keep her marks up so she could get into the college of her choice.

Caroline felt as if her world was falling in on her. She lost her enthusiasm for things she normally enjoyed. She had no motivation at school and couldn't focus. Even though she was exhausted, she couldn't sleep; she would lie awake all night thinking about everything. And although she had always loved food, she couldn't eat, she had completely lost her appetite. She started having difficulty going to school and often had to call her mom to come and get her.

After a long talk with her mom, Caroline agreed to go see her family doctor, who diagnosed her as being depressed, put her on an antidepressant, and sent her to see a counselor. At first, the medication made Caroline feel pretty nauseous, but after a couple of weeks she got used to it. The combination of the medication and talking with her counselor really helped.

Being diagnosed as depressed was difficult for Caroline. She felt guilty that she had to be on medication to feel better, and would compare herself with others who seemed much worse off than herself. It took a while for her to understand that, even though there are people with bigger problems, she needed a bit of extra help to get through hers.

Caroline has just finished her first year in college and is looking forward to the future. She knows that depression is something she will probably have to deal with all her life, but she feels strong enough now to handle it. As she says, "Once you've been through it and you're able to get out of it, then you can handle pretty much anything."

DEFINITION OF DEPRESSION

"When I'm depressed, I always think that I'm stupid. I sometimes wish that I had never existed." Robert, 9

Depression is not something anyone looks forward to, but it is something everyone experiences in one form or another. You may have felt kind of low or bummed out after you scored badly on a test; you may have been really sad after you broke up with your girl-friend or boyfriend; or you may have been completely dejected when you didn't make the team you had your heart set on. All of these

are important experiences that can affect our moods and ultimately our sense of self-worth. Feeling sad and/or mad is a natural and healthy response when a bad thing happens. As humans, we are privileged to have access to a range of emotions that make us both interesting and complex.

THERE ARE MANY DIFFERENT KINDS OF SAD.

These normal and healthy reactions are called **reactive depression**. This is depression that can be linked to a specific event and does not last more than a few days to a few weeks. It affects our mood in that it may make us grumpy, irritable, and often sad. This kind of depression is not considered a mental illness, and is the most common form of depression among adolescents.

"In my experience, depression is the fluctuation of moods. Everybody gets sad and everybody gets happy. I think depression is a continuation of being sad and lonely and feeling unwanted." Clifford, 18

There is another kind of depression that not everyone experiences and that hits much harder. This is referred to as **clinical depression**. It is estimated that one in five adolescents in the U.S. experiences clinical depression. This kind of depression can last a long time (months or years if not treated properly) and many people who experience it have to learn how to manage it throughout their whole lives.

CHECK IT OUT page 151

"The easiest way to explain it is to say he never got out of the 'terrible twos.' Through grades 3, 4, and 5, he would just get really bad tempers, especially around doing things like homework. He would

get very, very frustrated and would end up storming off to his room and slamming his door. By the time he was eight, he was slamming his door and screaming that he was going to kill himself. That's when we took him to a psychiatrist. That's when we thought, 'Oh, this isn't normal. This isn't just moodiness.' That's when we thought, 'This is a problem.'" Maria and George, parents

"I think I realized I was depressed when, instead of thinking I was a happy person who had a few bumps in the road at times, I thought of myself as an extremely unhappy person who some- times had a few good days. The bad outnumbered the good by so much that I would lie in bed at night and be surprised when I thought, 'Hey, today was an okay day.'" Susan, 19

In the world of mental health, clinical depression is classified as a **mood disorder**. This means that it is more than moodiness— it is an illness that alters your moods in a significant way. Some other mood disorders include anxiety disorders and bipolar disorder, which are both explored in the coming chapters.

RISK FACTORS FOR DEPRESSION

A **risk factor** is something that you have or something that happens to you that increases your chances of being affected by a certain issue. Researchers have come up with some risk factors that are common among adolescents who have been diagnosed with clinical depression: having a parent with depression, having an anxiety disorder, being female, and experiencing a traumatic life event. If one or more of these factors is present, it may increase your chances of having depression, but it does not automatically mean that you will. Most probably, it would be a combination of these factors (perhaps a genetic predisposition combined with a traumatic life event) that would trigger depression in you. Even if you have all four major risk factors for depression, you may never experience it. They are just common threads that weave the complicated picture of adolescent depression together.

Parent with Depression (Genetics)

As mentioned earlier, adolescent depression is a relatively new discovery. Issues such as adolescent suicide, eating disorders, and self-mutilation have doctors, parents, and researchers trying to figure out what's wrong. Some believe that the reason more and more adolescents are suffering from depression (especially bipolar disorder) is, in part, what they call the "cohort effect."

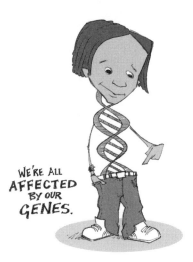

WE'RE ALL AFFECTED BY OUR GENES.

We know that depression is partly due to genetics. What is being discovered is that these genetic features may be mutating from generation to generation, making them stronger and more invasive earlier on in a person's life. So, while your parent may not have been affected by depression until their twenties, these inherited genes may start working in you as early as 10. This 10-year leap backwards is the "cohort effect." Remember, though, that depression is not only about genetics; stressful life situations can play a big part. And just because your parent suffers from depression, it's not necessarily true that you will too.

Anxiety Disorder

Anxiety also plays a major role in depression, especially with adolescents. An anxiety disorder is often characterized by an uncontrollable fear of either specific things (for example, spiders) or general issues (life and death). An anxiety disorder is different from being nervous or a bit worried—it can control your life. Feeling scared and overwhelmed by the world can lead to a depression that keeps you from enjoying life. For more information on the link between anxiety disorders and depression, see chapter 4.

ANXIETY

"I think my depression is a by-product of my anxiety, because I find myself worrying and thinking about things first, then that leads me to becoming depressed. I'll be worried about a paper or a project that I have to do, and as things build up I sort of start feeling crummy and start to avoid things." Simon, 21

Being Female

Don't panic if you're a girl reading this. This is just a risk factor—not a life sentence. Adolescent girls experience depression almost twice as often as adolescent boys. While no one is really sure why this is, there are many ideas about the probable causes. These are explored further in chapter 8.

Traumatic Life Event

When bad things happen in the world or to you personally, it's hard not to be negative about it. It's doubly hard not to feel bad about yourself when something happens that hurts your feelings or breaks your heart. Depression is often described as anger turned inwards. This means that we take the anger that we have towards the world, our families, our friends, or specific life events and we turn it against ourselves. Instead of saying "That sucks," someone who is depressed might say, "That happened because I suck."

"Watching the news and all the bad things that go on I seem to take worse than most people. I become pessimistic about everything. Usually I like company, but I just want to be alone when I'm depressed. It's scary sometimes." Ernesto, 20

Traumatic life events are un-avoidable. We all experience them on some level—whether they happen to us directly or we witness them through media images. They make us feel vulnerable and they bring the possibility of disaster directly to our lives. It's important to remember that there is a lot of good in the world (the  media loves to report the negative!). It's also important to surround yourself with friends and family who love you when you are feeling low. They can remind you how great you really are.

"All I really, really need is for someone to really have faith in me, to show me I can do things. It would encourage me to do it more." Isabel, 22

COMMON TRIGGERS FOR DEPRESSION

SEASONS CHANGE

Triggers for depression include changes in the seasons or in time (for example, when the clocks move ahead an hour in spring), transitions in school, and major life events such as divorce, illness, or death. Many people who suffer from depression know that when the seasons change or when they face a transition in life, they may feel particularly low. Once you start getting help and talking with people about how you feel, you may find out that things that have happened in your life have actually contributed to how you feel today. When you figure out what kinds of things might trigger depression in you, you can learn to tackle them head-on and prepare yourself for what lies ahead.

WHEN YOU LEAST EXPECT IT

Raymond's mother suffers from depression (genetics) and his favorite grandparent, whom he was extremely close to, died recently (traumatic life event). Although his risk factors are high, he will not necessarily be sidelined by depression. He may carry on with his life, feeling a bit sad but doing okay. A year later, however, when he starts at a new school, he may find himself unable to get out of bed and swamped by depression. In this example, although he had gone through a tough time earlier, the trigger for Raymond's depression was actually the transition to a new school a year later.

"It started for me when I was in grade 10, so I must have been 14 or 15 when I started feeling a little different from how I'd normally felt. As a child I'd always been pretty quiet, but normal. In grade 10, I started to— I don't know to this day exactly what it was. I remember having a feeling of not wanting to go to school at all that winter. I couldn't get out of bed. I was trying to avoid everything." Simon, 21

SYMPTOMS OF CLINICAL DEPRESSION

"To me, depression is not wanting to do anything—nothing is worth your time. It's pretty much just being really sad, or almost lazy to someone else, but to you, you just feel like you can't do anything. It almost feels like you can't move or something." Charlie, 13

Clinical depression affects each person so differently that it can be difficult to diagnose, especially in adolescents. As a teenager you are almost *expected* to be moody and unhappy, and the symptoms of depression are very similar to the symptoms of adolescent moodiness. What makes it even harder to diagnose is that each person's symptoms are different. One person may sleep a lot while another doesn't sleep at all. Some people will eat more and some will refuse to eat. Some people will be very tearful and feeling sad all the time, while others don't feel anything—they can participate in activities but have no feeling about them.

There are three characteristics that most doctors look for when they diagnose someone with depression. They are **persistence** (your sadness lasts longer than two weeks), **pervasiveness** (you have all or most of the symptoms listed on page 51), and **functional impairment** (you are unable to manage your day-to-day life).

THINGS JUST AREN'T **FUN**.

"I think my depression is not only being sad and crying and stuff, it's more not being able to be happy. You may be having fun and laughing and stuff, but you're never totally happy ... it's like there's a base missing, like something has fallen out. There's always this hole in your happiness that's making everything kind of screwed up." Claire, 17

"Even now, I have no ambition about anything. Everything either doesn't interest me or only interests me a little bit ... I don't want anything. I'm sure it has to do with the depression. I'm just not passionate about anything." Isabel, 22

"I think it [depression] is the overall avoidance of everyday things and a lack of motivation to go on and do the things you want to do and have the relationships you want to have. That's what it is to me, the overall emptiness and sadness you feel, and the lack of desire." Simon, 21

The symptoms of clinical depression are related to specific things, including sleeping and eating and feeling. Any changes in your feelings, behavior, or habits that last more than two weeks may be a sign that you are depressed.

SOME SIGNS OF DEPRESSION

- ◆ Sadness
- ◆ Irritability
- ◆ Not able to have fun
- ◆ Spending less time with friends
- ◆ Sleeping too much or too little
- ◆ Loss of appetite or increased appetite
- ◆ Loss of energy
- ◆ Difficulty concentrating
- ◆ Low self-esteem
- ◆ Frequent thoughts of death/suicide

WARNING

Any thoughts or talk of suicide must be taken seriously. If you are feeling suicidal, you must find someone to talk to *now*. If your friend is talking about suicide, you need to get the help of an adult right away. This is not something you should deal with on your own. Don't keep it to yourself even if your friend has asked you not to tell anyone. Better to have an angry friend than a dead one. Don't keep it a secret!

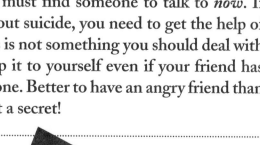

"I honestly felt scared that if I got out of bed and went to school, something really bad would happen—not that I would get injured, but that I would feel emotionally hurt by something, somehow. I can remember certain times when I was just scared of everything. I was scared of dying and scared of living. I had times of uncontrollable crying. I couldn't stop. I wasn't crying about anything specific, just overall terrible feelings." Simon, 21

"You keep your eyes open when you're depressed so you can spot anything that's wrong and against you, then you go, 'See that? They're on his side. Life is unfair.' And you point out anything you wouldn't normally notice." Ella, 12

"When I'm depressed, I don't talk much; I just listen to everyone else. I get restless and can't stay in one place for too long. I continuously change my mind about what I need to be doing to distract myself, but usually nothing works, so I get reclusive." Isabel, 22

"When I'm depressed, I feel mad and I always try to launch my anger and depression towards something else, or someone else in some cases. You can really tell when your mood changes. Somehow you feel there's something inside you that you need to let out because you can't handle it anymore. It's a feeling sort of like a sick feeling, because you really want to act and behave normally, but there's something that's bothering you and you just have to launch it at someone or something." Victor, 18

DIFFERENCES BETWEEN ADULTS AND ADOLESCENTS

Depression is pretty much the same for an adolescent as it is for an adult, but some of the symptoms can be different. Adults usually experience what is called **classic depression**, while adolescents are more likely to experience **atypical depression**.

For example, adolescents who are depressed are able to break free of that depression at times and actually go out and have fun with a group of friends. Adults often find it hard to muster up the energy to go out when they are depressed. This makes it even harder for an adult to tell if you're depressed, because when you are, you don't necessarily behave the way they would.

Adolescents are more difficult to treat for depression. They are less likely to take their medication regularly as they worry that it will alter their personality and change who they really are, just when they are figuring that out for themselves. They may also be more reluctant to talk about how they feel, especially with an adult, as they often feel misunderstood by adults in general. This can mean that adolescents don't always get the treatment they need and that their depression can take longer to get under control.

"I admit I don't always take my medication regularly. It's usually when I'm at home for the summer with my friends, when I don't have any tests or quizzes and things are fairly simple. People who are close to me, mostly my mom, can immediately tell when I'm not on my medication because there's that much of a difference in me. I too notice a difference, but not as much as those around me do." Susan, 19

There are social issues for adolescents that can also affect their ability to get treatment and to stick with it. As discussed in chapter 2, school is a really important factor in the life of an adolescent, and for most it's impossible to escape. By contrast, adults can often take time off work when they are ill and then pick up where they left off once they have recovered. An adolescent who needs to take time off may fall behind in school and even lose a year to the illness. This means that when they have recovered, they don't pick up where they left off; they often have to make new friends, change schools, and repeat the grade that they missed. Remember, though, that correspondence school or part-time studies can take some of the pressure off and give you the time you need to focus on getting better.

CORRESPONDENCE...

"Being behind in school is the most stressful thing in the world. It's strange how that can happen, because school is just school—it's not like, if you fail, you're going to die—but definitely school is a big thing. School isn't like a job. School moves at such a pace that you can't take time off and then come back: you'll be behind and you'll be too old." Claire, 17

SEASONAL AFFECTIVE DISORDER (SAD)

On a cold and dreary fall afternoon everything can seem depressing. For some people, the winter months can trigger a real depression that lasts until the spring or summer. This is called

Seasonal Affective Disorder (SAD). SAD is a mood disorder that causes symptoms of depression that are related to seasonal changes in light. In the fall and winter, when the days become shorter and it starts to get dark earlier, SAD can take hold.

"I've never felt depressed in the summer. It always seems to happen between November and March, so it might have something to do with the weather, or the lack of light."
Simon, 21

In darkness (usually while we sleep) our bodies produce a hormone called melatonin. High levels of melatonin have been linked with depression. When the winter sets in, the days get shorter and we get less daylight, and our levels of melatonin rise.

SAD has become a well-recognized condition in North America and around the world. There are a variety of products that have been developed to help people feel better, including special lights that give off a lot more brightness than regular bulbs, and alarm clocks that wake you up gently by increasing the light in your room (like the sun rising). It may be that all the time we spend indoors, watching TV, working, or playing video games, has a negative impact on us. In previous generations, kids spent much more time outside, playing and

THE FOUR MAIN TYPES OF CLINICAL DEPRESSION

Major Depressive Disorder (also called Major Depression)
- A severe depression
- In adolescents, it lasts on average from seven to nine months.

Dysthymic Disorder (also called Dysthymia or Mild Depression)
- A milder but more chronic (long-lasting) form of depression
- The most common form of depression experienced by adolescents
- Low-level depression that is felt most of the day, most days, for many years
- In adolescents, the average duration is four years – some kids spend their entire adolescence depressed.

Double Depression
- A combination of Major Depressive Disorder and Dysthymia
- A depression that is both severe and chronic

Bipolar Disorder (Also known as Manic Depression)
- Characterized by unusual shifts in mood and energy

55

GET OUTSIDE

hanging out. They helped on the family farm after school or rode around on their bikes with their friends. Television, computers, and video games have brought us indoors and keep us there, depriving us of precious daylight. We may also be so concerned about skin cancer that we hide from the sun rather than bask in it. But you don't have to sunbathe to get the positive effects of light.

CHECK IT OUT
page 152

So don't just sit there, get outside and soak up that daylight (safely, that is).

AN UNWELCOME VISITOR

When you're depressed, it can be hard to separate yourself from your depression. But remember, depression isn't who you are, it's something that is happening to you. Whether it's caused by genetics, a life trauma, or no apparent reason at all, it's not your fault.

"When you're diagnosed as someone with depression, someone who is sad or upset all the time is what you consider your usual self. I was so upset for so long that I just took on an identity as an angry, emotional person. Being diagnosed with depression doesn't mean you're some crazy person or something. It just means that there is a problem in you that is very difficult to control on your own, and you probably need some help." Susan, 19

Feeling as if you are alone in your depression is common, and so is feeling guilty for being depressed. You may think that people won't understand what you are feeling because they seem to have bigger problems than you have.

"I had a lot of guilt about being depressed. Going on the medication was like, 'Aren't there people with more problems, yet they're putting me on a pill because I'm feeling sad?' I felt really pathetic." Caroline, 19

AN UNWELCOME VISITOR

"It's more the guilt and the pressure that makes the whole experience worse. Everybody would be trying to get me to go to school, but I'd just be crying and I just couldn't do it. I felt like such a failure." Isabel, 22

It is important to remember that you are not alone. You also need to keep in mind that everybody's problems are relative; each of our experiences are real and true to us. There are so many people out there who can help you out, if you just let them know what you are going through. Chances are they have felt some of the same things too.

"It's a good idea to run your thoughts on it by someone else who is close to you, like your parents or siblings. Because chances are, if you've noticed that something is wrong, they've probably noticed too." Susan, 19

WHAT TO DO NEXT

If you think you might be depressed, talking about it is the best place to start. Find someone you trust—a friend, a family member, a teacher, a neighbor—and let them know. You don't have to get into a huge, detailed conversation right off the bat. You just need to let someone know so that you can share your burden and so that you know someone is looking out for you. This person can help you find a counselor or other professional who is trained to treat your depression. For more information on what kinds of help are available, see chapter 10.

"There are things that help, but they don't make everything okay. There's nothing specific they can say, because they can only help me so much. I have to just feel it and talk about it myself. Another part of your brain is working [when you are depressed], so stuff comes out that you don't even know you're feeling until you start talking about it. So, I think just having someone who will listen, who will let me say whatever I want to say, helps." Simon, 21

If you think you have a friend or sibling who might be depressed, here's some advice from people who have been through it.

Things you shouldn't do or say if you think someone you know is depressed:

"I think the worst thing someone can do when I'm depressed is compare me to someone else ... Sometimes it's helpful to hear others' stories so that you know you're not alone. But more often than not, comparing me to someone else makes my feelings seem insignificant— kind of like everyone has them, and why do I think that I am so special that I should be allowed to be upset over those things? I hate when people start trying to find solutions for me the moment I have

finished telling them what is wrong. If you have answers right off the bat, it makes me feel like either you weren't listening at all or that my problems are minor and I'm overreacting." Susan, 19

"The one thing that always infuriates me is when they say, 'I understand what you're going through.' Don't say it." Mary, 21

"For people who have friends who are depressed, don't try telling them they are depressed. 'Cause you know it's true, or some part of your brain knows it's true, even if you don't know it yet, and of course you don't want anybody to know you're depressed—well, at the beginning—and you especially don't want your best friend telling you that you're depressed." Ella, 12

"We had a counselor in our school and she would come up to me in front of everybody and put her arm around my shoulder and say, 'How are you feeling?' Don't do that in front of everybody! It was really humiliating. So, people pushing too hard doesn't help. When you're really depressed, you have to feel ready to talk to somebody. It's good that people push you a little bit, so you know they're there when you need help, but constantly nagging at somebody … Or the people who dealt with it as though it wasn't anything serious, like it was just all in your head … In a way, it is all in your head, but it's very real for the person who's going through it." Caroline, 19

Things you can do or say that might help:

"Just let me be upset for a while. Nod your head, and then maybe you can tell me what you think I should do about it. More often than not, I know the answer, but I just need someone to vent to." Susan, 19

"Sometimes when my mom would tell me that I'm not really depressed or I'm just feeling like I am, it makes me feel better, even if I am depressed." Robert, 9

"Do be really understanding. Provide comfort, provide a sense of security, because it's something that's really lacking. At that point say, 'It's okay. We're going to get through this. We are standing by you and we're going to go through this with you. We're here to offer whatever help and comfort you need.'" Mary, 21

"Listen to your kid. Listen. Don't preach, don't try to cheer them up too much. Listen, listen, listen." Maria, parent

Chapter 4
Depression and Anxiety: Panic and Fear

Many adolescents who experience anxiety may also have depression. In fact, anxiety is one of the most common issues associated with depression. This chapter explores what an anxiety disorder is and how it is different from everyday anxiety. It also explains how anxiety is linked to depression, especially in adolescents.

In grade 10, Marlee started to have severe anxiety attacks. She would be sitting in class and become so panicked that she would have to get up and run out of the room. Many times she got so anxious that she would hyperventilate and pass out. Eventually she was diagnosed with depression and an anxiety disorder. Her doctor started her on antidepressants and sent her to see a counselor. Through counseling she realized that she had been suffering from anxiety for most of her life.

She remembers that in grade 2 she started having bad headaches and stomach aches. When she was asked to read out loud to the class, she became so anxious that she couldn't speak. She eventually told her teacher that she couldn't see, so she ended up with glasses she didn't really need. She would have sudden jolts of "physical anxiety and extreme worry" over things that she knew were irrational, such as thinking that she had forgotten to get dressed. She also had a lot of anxiety around her peers and worried that she did not fit in. Her anxiety made her an easy target for the "cool" kids, who often shot her down and picked on her. This only increased her anxiety. Marlee has some good friends now who understand her well, but she has had a lot of difficulty with boyfriends. She needs a lot of reassurance and attention to make her feel secure.

Marlee experiences real physical reactions to stress in her life, from feeling nauseous to passing out. When she is anxious, she is unable to enjoy things that would otherwise be pleasant because she cannot stop her worries from creeping into her mind. She has had many suicidal thoughts, has been diagnosed with an eating disorder, and for a brief period was cutting herself. It has been a rough road for Marlee, but she has a great relationship with her counselor, whom she has been seeing since grade 10. She is no longer on antidepressants but wishes that she could feel "normal" more often.

Marlee is working hard at becoming a social worker, and amazingly, her stressful career choice has been a bit of a distraction for her. "I think about whatever I'm worrying about pretty consistently. Today I was in a meeting for three hours and I didn't think about it for three hours, and it was like a vacation when I realized it."

EVERYDAY ANXIETY

Everyone experiences anxiety at some point. You notice the girl or boy you really like walking towards you, and you can feel your heart racing and your palms get sweaty. Just the thought of having to talk to this person sends you into an anxiety-induced stupor. Or maybe you have been working all week on your class project and today is the day you have to perform. As you listen to your classmate wrap up their presentation, you know your turn is next. Just the idea of getting up in front of the class is making you feel incredibly nauseous. It's your turn. You get up slowly from your chair, walk to the front of the class, and turn to face everyone.

Your cheeks are burning. You open your mouth, but nothing comes out. Your anxiety has swallowed your voice—it ate your report!

As painful as they are, these are all normal responses to stressful situations. Once the stressful situation has passed, you return to your regular self—embarrassed, but generally unscathed. You can laugh about it with your friends, because they've all been through it.

"Everything I've been learning to do is about distinguishing normal anxiety from not-normal anxiety. A person suffering from an anxiety disorder gets both, and it's really important to be able to distinguish which is which." Mary, 21

THE LINK BETWEEN ANXIETY AND DEPRESSION

Depression and anxiety often show up together in adolescents. In fact, almost 50 percent of teenagers who have clinical depression are also likely to suffer from an anxiety disorder. No one's really sure whether depression causes anxiety or anxiety triggers depression, although 85 percent of teenagers who have both anxiety and depression say they experienced anxiety first. Research has also shown that many of the same nerve pathways and brain regions are involved in both depression and anxiety. For this reason, doctors often prescribe antidepressants for their patients with anxiety disorders even if they are not clinically depressed.

"Usually the anxiety triggers the depression. The anxiety is always there. That's just how I am, and I can usually cope with it. When I become too anxious, I begin to feel depressed." Ernesto, 20

THE FIVE MAJOR TYPES OF ANXIETY DISORDER

Generalized Anxiety Disorder (GAD)

An uncontrollable fear of the future and worry about ability and performance. Someone with GAD may be irritable and restless, have trouble sleeping, and be extremely self-critical.

Social Phobia

Extreme self-consciousness that leads to a fear of social or performance situations. It is often accompanied by physical symptoms such as sweating, heart palpitations, or shortness of breath. Individuals with social phobia may have low self-esteem and be overly sensitive to criticism. They will often avoid situations that make them anxious (for example, skip school or avoid social outings with friends).

Obsessive Compulsive Disorder (OCD)

Frequent and uncontrollable thoughts (obsessions) that lead to routines and rituals (compulsions) in an effort to get rid of the thoughts. Someone with OCD will repeat behaviors (wash hands repeatedly, turn lights on and off) in order to avoid some imagined consequence. This can take up so much time that it seriously interferes with the person's ability to function on a daily basis.

Post-Traumatic Stress Disorder

Persistent and frightening thoughts of a traumatic event that has happened. Someone with post-traumatic stress disorder may experience extreme anxiety as they relive a traumatic event that they have experienced or witnessed, such as a rape or murder, a natural disaster, or an act of war. These memories may disturb their sleep with nightmares, and they may become irritable, aggressive, and even violent.

Panic Disorder

Unexplained and repeated episodes of intense fear (panic attacks), which are often accompanied by physical symptoms such as chest pain, heart palpitations, irritable bowel syndrome, and dizziness. Someone with panic disorder may become very anxious between attacks, worrying about when the next one will happen.

ANXIETY DISORDERS

Anxiety that interferes with your life and keeps you from doing the things you once enjoyed is not "everyday." This kind of anxiety can take over your life and make you miserable.

CHECK IT OUT
page 153

"Whenever I'm faced with any sort of important decisions, I'll try to avoid it as much as possible because I don't want to make the wrong one. Choices about anything, even something like what style to do my room in—I'm so afraid it might be not what I really like, that I'm just being influenced by other people. Things plague me that wouldn't plague other people." Isabel, 22

SOME COMMON TRIGGERS FOR ANXIETY INCLUDE:

• exposure to the thing that makes you anxious (a crowd of people, a spider)
• pressure at school (exams)
• a traumatic life event (such as a death or illness)

CROWDS

PANIC ATTACKS

A panic attack is an intense experience, and for some people it can happen any time and anywhere. Maybe you're lying on the couch at home, watching TV, when all of a sudden you feel panicked. Your heart is racing, and even though you don't know why, you are certain that something bad is going to happen.

"I felt severe anxiety. I can't really put my finger on what it is. It's like you feel trapped but there's nothing really there." Ernesto, 20

SYMPTOMS OF A PANIC ATTACK MAY INCLUDE:

◆ a feeling of intense fear or impending doom

◆ palpitations or increased heart rate

◆ sweating, shaking, and a dry mouth

◆ difficulty breathing

◆ a feeling of choking

◆ chest pain

◆ nausea, or abdominal pain

◆ numbness or tingling in hands, feet, or around the mouth

◆ dizziness

◆ a fear that you are going to pass out or that you are dying

The first time you have a panic attack can be really frightening. You may feel that you are dying. If you have a panic attack in a certain place, you may be afraid to go back there for fear of it happening again. Having a panic attack does not mean you are going crazy, it's just your body's response to some mixed-up messages in your brain. Researchers are not sure what exactly causes panic attacks, but they think that for some reason your brain is giving your body the message that it is under attack. This may be related to genetics, stressful life events, or other hereditary factors.

page 153

"My usual self almost is my depressed self, but I have moments of lucidity. That's what I would like my usual self to be. When I'm depressed or anxiety-ridden, or both at the same time, which I think is pretty much it, I feel like I'm crazy. It's hard to separate those two things. I can look at everything I'm saying and say, 'That's crazy' but I can't not feel it. So I can think what is logical, but I can't believe it's true, so I feel crazy when I'm depressed and anxious."
Marlee, 21

Each year, 2.4 million Americans experience panic disorder. Women are twice as likely as men to develop the disorder. Panic disorder usually strikes in young adulthood. Roughly half of all people who have panic disorder develop the condition before age 24.

YOU ARE WHAT YOU EAT (AND SMOKE)

- Caffeine can cause symptoms of anxiety and panic attacks. Caffeine is found in many of your favorite foods and beverages, including soft drinks, chocolate bars, and ice cream.
- Many people report that their first panic attack happened when they got high on marijuana.
- Using drugs such as marijuana, cocaine, and amphetamines can cause symptoms of depression and anxiety.

SPECIFIC PHOBIAS

We all have fears and worries in our lives. Some people don't like to fly, some people are terrified of snakes, some people feel anxious in crowded places. These fears and worries are not a serious problem as long as they do not keep you from participating in life. So, if your fear of flying is so great that you can't get on the plane to go to your family reunion, or if your fear of snakes keeps you from ever going anywhere where you might run into one (camp, the country, the basement), then your fear might just be a phobia.

The anxiety that goes with a phobia is so overwhelming that your body almost shuts down. This is due to a natural response to stressful situations that has been with us since our days as cave dwellers. It's a basic animal instinct designed to keep us alive: fight or flight. When you have a phobia, that flight instinct takes over in a big way, producing a physical response that makes it impossible for you to put yourself in contact with what you're afraid of even if you know your fear is irrational.

SOME SPECIFIC PHOBIAS ◀ • • • • • • • • • • • •

Acrophobia	fear of heights
Apiphobia	fear of bees
Arachnophobia	fear of spiders
Brontophobia	fear of thunder and lightning
Cynophobia	fear of dogs and rabies
Elurophobia	fear of cats
Entomophobia	fear of insects
Ophidiophobia	fear of snakes
Trypanophobia	fear of injections
Verminophobia	fear of germs

INSECTS

Please remember that for people who have a phobia, exposure to the thing they are afraid of can cause an extreme reaction. So, while it may seem funny to dangle a worm in front of your friend's face and hear her scream, it may not be so funny to her. It may cause her to panic.

DOGS

The good news about anxiety and phobias is that they are fairly easy to treat. Treatment can include desensitization (exposing you to what you are afraid of, in small doses over a long period of time, helping you to get used to it), cognitive behavior therapy (teaching you to control your thoughts and anxieties), and in some cases anti-anxiety or antidepressant medication. For more information on treatments and therapies, see chapter 10.

THINGS YOU CAN DO IF YOU ARE WITH SOMEONE WHO IS HAVING A PANIC ATTACK

◆ Encourage them to take deep breaths from the diaphragm. This will keep them from hyperventilating and possibly passing out.

◆ Encourage them to visualize a calm and safe place. This will help to relax them.

◆ Once they have calmed down, encourage them to talk to a counselor or adult who can help figure out what is going on.

Advice on what NOT to do, from someone who's been through it

"I find people telling me there's no reason to be scared is absolutely useless and a bit frustrating. You sit there going, 'Yeah, I know that,' but the big thing about fear and anxiety is that they are not logical. It's not about what makes sense, so people trying to reason with you, telling you you're being silly, is a) not helpful and b) hurtful, because it is how you feel and there's nothing you can do about it." Mary, 21

Chapter 5
Bipolar Disorder: Highs and Lows

Bipolar disorder (also known as manic depression) is a mood disorder that affects over 2 million adults in America. Chances are, many of these adults were bipolar as adolescents. The dramatic changes in mood that swing from depression to mania and that are at the core of this illness can be hard to separate from adolescent moodiness. This chapter explores what it means to be bipolar and how it may affect your life. It also highlights some important facts that any adolescent who is bipolar should be aware of.

Charlie had always been an anxious child. He had a lot of trouble separating from his parents and missed 30 days of school in his first year of kindergarten. His parents would have to drag him into the classroom kicking and screaming. As he grew older, his anxiety got worse and he had trouble controlling his temper. He often flew into a rage over small things. When he was about 10, Charlie's anxiety started to get really out of control. He would get ready for school, leave the house, but then turn around and come back. He just couldn't make himself go—he was sure something bad was going to happen.

Instead of going to school, Charlie would stay at home and play on the computer, isolating himself from the world outside. His parents tried everything they could to help him. He started to have serious trouble controlling his temper, and became very aggressive. He saw many doctors, but most of them just thought he was acting out. His mother suffers from bipolar disorder, and she knew that something more was going on. She recognized some of her own symptoms of mania and depression in Charlie. Finally, one doctor diagnosed Charlie with depression and prescribed an antidepressant. The anti-

depressant plunged Charlie into a severe manic state. His rages became uncontrollable, he stopped sleeping, and his depression mounted.

As his mother described, "By this time, we were having daily episodes where he was psychotic. He would kind of sing, and talk in baby talk. That was one of the warnings, for us, that it was about to happen. He was psychotic, and he would talk about killing himself. He was attacking himself and us with knives, he was attacking the cats. It was almost like a blind rage that he would get into. He was very, very strong for the duration of it, he had an uncommon strength —and it would go two or three hours. I could barely hold him down. When it was over, he would just be himself again. He would be so sorry. He'd be very apologetic and we'd all just be exhausted, and he wouldn't remember anything of what happened for that two or three hours."

More than once his parents had to call the police to take him to the hospital because he was so out of control. Several doctors and many agonizing months later, Charlie found the right doctor, the right therapy program, and the right combination of medications.

Charlie has been diagnosed as bipolar with an anxiety disorder. Charlie and his mom both agree that they can set each other off with their moods and they have to watch out for that, but life at home is finally calm. After missing over two years of school, Charlie is now back with his friends in grade 8. He understands that his illness is something he will have to pay attention to all his life, and he has the support of his family to help him along the way.

As an adolescent you probably get pretty moody, and in any given day you might go from really happy to bummed out and back to happy again without really thinking about it. This is fine and normal (for both adolescents and adults) because life can be a roller coaster of emotions. There is a condition, though, that takes that ride to an extreme: bipolar disorder (also called **manic depression**). This is an illness that makes a person's moods, thoughts, and energy change dramatically.

CHECK IT OUT
page 153

Someone who is bipolar may swing from a low mood (depression) to a high mood (mania) several times a day. These lows and highs can also last for days, weeks, or months. When people with bipolar disorder are low, they feel depressed—just like the depression discussed in chapter 3. When they are high, they can feel irritable, invincible, speedy, and unstoppable.

"She [my doctor] told me that I had extremely low lows and extremely high highs, but there was no gray zone in between them. She explained that my brain just had trouble balancing them, and that my lows and highs were more extreme than they should have been." Susan, 19

BIPOLAR DISORDER IN CHILDREN AND ADOLESCENTS

Bipolar disorder is a complicated condition that can be very difficult to diagnose, especially in children and adolescents. In children, many of the symptoms of bipolar disorder (irritability, rages, hyperactivity) are often mistaken for other disorders, such as Attention Deficit Disorder (ADD). In adolescents, many of the symptoms (irritability, emotional outbursts) are mistaken for adolescent moodiness. So how do you know if someone's bipolar or just plain moody? It can be hard to tell, but generally, adolescent moodiness is milder and less dramatic than the highs and lows of bipolar disorder.

GRANDIOSE DELUSIONS

IN BIPOLAR DISORDER, THE SYMPTOMS OF MANIA INCLUDE:

◆ increased physical and mental activity and energy

◆ heightened mood, exaggerated optimism and self-confidence

◆ excessive irritability, aggressive behavior

◆ decreased need for sleep without experiencing fatigue

◆ grandiose delusions, inflated sense of self-importance

◆ racing speech, racing thoughts, flight of ideas

◆ impulsiveness, poor judgment, distractibility

◆ reckless behavior

◆ in the most severe cases, delusions and hallucinations

"I remember thinking, 'I can do anything. I don't care what anyone says.' This wasn't mad, this was strong—it was a feeling of being king and no one could stop you …You have this really good feeling, even if you know it's wrong. You have this really good feeling and this tension which lifts you up and everything, so you think you can do anything, like mouthy things or being mean to everybody, but you think you can get away with it." Ella, 12

IN BIPOLAR DISORDER, THE SYMPTOMS OF DEPRESSION INCLUDE:

◆ prolonged sadness or unexplained crying spells

◆ significant changes in appetite and sleep patterns

◆ irritability, anger, worry, agitation, anxiety

◆ pessimism, indifference

◆ loss of energy, persistent lethargy

◆ feelings of guilt, worthlessness

◆ inability to concentrate, indecisiveness

◆ inability to take pleasure in former interests, social withdrawal

◆ unexplained aches and pains

◆ recurring thoughts of death or suicide

WARNING

Any thoughts or talk of suicide must be taken seriously. If you are feeling suicidal, you must find someone to talk to *now*. If your friend is talking about suicide, you need to get the help of an adult right away. This is not something you should deal with on your own. Don't keep it to yourself even if your friend has asked you not to tell anyone. Better to have an angry friend than a dead one. Don't keep it a secret!

"A lot of times when I am depressed, I am suicidal. But it's suicidal in a different kind of way, because I could never actually kill myself. It's more like I wish something awful would happen to me, like I could get hit by a car and killed or something, so that people wouldn't count me as some statistic for teenagers who take their own lives." Susan, 19

GENETIC RISK IN BIPOLAR DISORDER

Children with one parent who suffers from bipolar disorder have a 10 to 30 percent chance of developing the condition. Having a sibling with bipolar disorder means a 20 percent risk. If both parents have bipolar disorder, the risk can be as high as 75 percent. About 90 percent of people who have bipolar disorder have at least one relative with a mood disorder.

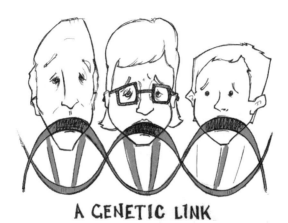

A GENETIC LINK

THE LINK BETWEEN DEPRESSION AND BIPOLAR DISORDER

It is estimated that one-third of children who are initially diagnosed with depression will develop bipolar disorder. It is important to know that the use of antidepressants by someone who is being treated for depression but is actually bipolar can throw them into a state of mania (like in Charlie's story). What does this mean for you? If you are depressed and seeking treatment, it's very important that you tell your doctor if you think there is a possibility that you are bipolar (for example, if you have a family history of bipolar disorder or if you have experienced some of the mood swings typical of bipolar disorder) before you take any antidepressant medication.

COMMON TRIGGERS FOR BIPOLAR DISORDER

People with bipolar disorder can often control it with proper medication and counseling, which will enable them to lead healthy and happy lives. Counseling can help them to understand their illness and to recognize common triggers that may negatively affect them. Some of the triggers for adolescents with bipolar disorder include:

◆ changes in seasons

◆ transitions in school or other life events

◆ traumatic life events

DIFFERENT TYPES OF BIPOLAR DISORDER

There are three major forms of bipolar disorder, which relate to how far and how fast your moods swing:

1. BPI—when your mood swings between severe mania and severe depression

2. BPII—when your mood swings between mild mania (**hypomania**) and severe depression

3. Cyclothymia—when your mood swings between mild mania and mild depression

Other characteristics of bipolar disorder:
Mixed state—when you experience symptoms of depression and mania together
Rapid cycling—when your mood changes from depression to mania in either direction many times during a week or even a day

DIAGNOSIS

As anyone who has a mood disorder will tell you, once you're diagnosed, your life will never be the same. This is not necessarily a bad thing. You may finally get the support and treatment you have needed for a long time. You may feel relieved that there is a medical explanation for the way you are feeling. It's important to understand that having a mood disorder is like having any other disease—it's not your fault, it's just something you've got.

A diagnosis may also be a real relief for your family. Because bipolar disorder can be so difficult to pinpoint in adolescents, it can be heart-wrenching for the people who love you. When people with bipolar disorder are manic, they can say and do things that deeply hurt the people who are close to them. They may threaten to kill them (and even try), tell them they hate them, and break and destroy things that are dear to them. Your parents may blame themselves for your behavior, and after a manic episode you could feel sad and guilty about that. Once a proper diagnosis is made and the right medications are working for you, your life will start to come back together.

"It's weird talking about it now because we've been all the way through, from the bottom to the top. Things have gone really well now, but I think that we've been through so much that I think we're a much stronger family. It was a lot of work, but I think in that sense we're better off than a lot of families that don't have to go through this, because we're all able to talk about anything, we're all on the same side, and we can work through anything." George, parent

GOOD TO KNOW

As an adolescent, there are some important things that you should know if you have been diagnosed with bipolar disorder. When you understand your illness and the impact it can have on your life, you are better equipped to face the challenges ahead. For information on treatment options see chapter 10.

FACTS

◆ People who suffer from bipolar disorder have an alcohol and drug abuse rate triple that of the rest of the population.

◆ For at least half of the people who have bipolar disorder, the condition goes untreated.

◆ School stress and the hormone rush in puberty can send the condition into overdrive.

◆ Stimulants (amphetamines, caffeine) can trigger the disorder and could account for the increase in children and adolescents with bipolar disorder.

◆ Changes in a person's schedule, lack of sleep, and seasonal changes can trigger bipolar disorder.

◆ Therapy that works for one patient will not necessarily work for another.

◆ The rate of suicide for those with bipolar disorder is higher than that for the rest of the population (about 20 percent).

COMEBACK ◀ •

◆ Avoid drugs and alcohol, plain and simple—your risk for addiction is too high. And if you're on medication, throwing drugs and alcohol into the mix can seriously mess you up.

◆ Don't avoid treatment. Bipolar disorder will not go away on its own. Get to know your symptoms. Read all you can about depression and mood disorders. You can be your own advocate for the best treatment and therapy.

◆ Understand your adolescent self. Stress at school and your changing body can trip you up.

◆ Eat well and regularly. Stay away from coffee and tea, sodas, chocolate, and caffeinated foods.

◆ Be consistent with your routines. Try to get up and go to bed at the same time every day. Get lots of sleep and be aware of the changing seasons so you can be ready—prepare yourself/ protect yourself.

◆ Shop around for the right doctor and the right medication. It can take a while to get the combination that works best for you.

◆ If you are feeling suicidal, you need to talk to someone. Find a friend whom you can trust, tell an adult who can help you.

Chapter 6
Lifestyle and Food:
Eating Disorders and Disordered Eating

Your lifestyle and eating habits can have a big impact on your mood. Eating well and getting enough rest are important factors in feeling good about yourself and the world around you. This chapter looks at adolescent lifestyles and food choices in relation to depression. It also explores the issue of eating disorders, which are not necessarily about food at all but have a lot to do with how people feel about themselves.

Heather has two siblings and was always a problem-free child. She is not sure how her eating disorder started, but she thinks it was related to the fact that she was struggling with depression. Her depression started when she was about 16, but she still can't pinpoint what exactly triggered it. She had lots of friends, lived in a happy home, and was doing well in school.

Her eating disorder started out as bulimia but quickly turned to anorexia. She began by making herself throw up after every meal, and then she just stopped eating. She is amazed that no one in her family noticed that something was wrong. She spent hours in the bathroom in the basement after every meal. She wonders what would have happened if someone had intervened—maybe things wouldn't have got so out of control. She had a ritual around eating: she chose one thing to eat each day, which she would make last as long as possible. She often chose an iced coffee as her only nourishment for the day. As things got worse, she still didn't reach out to anyone for help—she kept her problems hidden. Although no one in her family knew how depressed she really was, when she was 17 she decided to go away to boarding school, hoping that a change would make things better. It didn't—her depression stayed with her and her eating disorder got worse.

Heather was so thin that she still can't believe no one ever noticed that something was wrong with her—but no one ever said anything. She was failing tests at school because she was so malnourished that she couldn't stay awake in class. Finally, when things got really bad and she felt as if she couldn't handle it anymore, she called her parents and told them she didn't know what was wrong with her but that she needed to come home. By the time she got back from boarding school, she had lost 16 kg (35 pounds) on her already petite frame.

Back home, Heather's depression continued. She felt that everyone else in the world was happy but that she would never be. Finally, her mom made her a doctor's appointment at a local children's hospital. When she got there, they immediately put her in a wheelchair and admitted her to the eating disorder ward. She was stunned and tried to explain to the nurses that she had to leave—she had things to do, places to go. Even though she knew it, she was not ready to admit that she had a problem. Although her mother visited her every day for the month that she stayed in the eating disorder program, Heather remained terrified that a nurse would let it slip that she had an eating disorder. They never talked about it, so she assumed her mother never knew. And maybe if they didn't talk about it, it wasn't really true.

Heather returned home, but it would take another month-long stay at the same hospital and then a five-month stay at a residential treatment program before she really got better. Although her eating disorder is now under control, she still struggles with depression. She takes a daily antidepressant, which takes the edge off her depression and helps her cope with the stress of school and life in general. Although it took a while before they could easily talk about it, her family, and especially her mother, have been a huge support to her. Her mother always believed in her and told her that she would get better. That unwavering faith kept her focused on her recovery.

Heather knows that depression is something she will struggle with all her life, but she is confident that her battle with her eating disorder is behind her. "The way I gauge my recovery is by knowing that I could never go back to that, which isn't to say that I'm 100 percent okay. What is normal now, anyway?"

BAD HABITS

When you're in grade school, someone is usually watching out for you, making sure that you get enough healthy food to eat, that you get enough sleep, and that you bathe on a regular basis. Once you are an adolescent, you are expected to start taking responsibility for your personal hygiene and are probably expected to make your own lunch. Perhaps when you come home from school you are on your own, so your snacking options begin to grow. Where once you were offered fruit and juice for an after-school snack, now the fridge is yours.

Adolescents and teenagers tend to make some of the most unhealthy food choices of all. This is not entirely their fault. Food companies market fast, fried, frozen, microwavable treats directly at the 12-to-16-year-old crowd. You are their favorite consumers. They know that you have great influence on your parents when it comes to food, entertainment, and clothes, so if they can make you like it, chances are you can talk your parents into buying it.

CHECK IT OUT — page 154

As the supervision in your life starts to ease up, you have some important choices to make. There are three key things that are going to

You Are Their FAVORITE CONSUMERS.

affect how you feel and behave as an adolescent, and these same three things are directly under your control: eating, sleeping, and exercising.

It makes sense that if you skip breakfast, eat chips and cola for lunch, have candy for a snack, skip gym class, sit on the couch in front of the computer all evening at home, and stay up until midnight online with your friends, then you are going to feel sluggish, unmotivated, easily bummed out, and dreary. You need to find a balance. Having the freedom to make choices for yourself doesn't mean that you automatically have to make unhealthy choices. It's hard to change your eating habits once you have settled into them, and they can affect your health for a long time.

DISORDERED EATING VS. EATING DISORDERS

Each of us has had negative thoughts about our body at some point: "my hips are too big," "my thighs are too fat." While these may not be healthy attitudes, they are human, especially in the world we live in today. Unrealistic images of beauty and thinness come at us from every direction. Our responses to food are related to what we see around us. Our cultural obsession with food rivals our obsession with beauty. Food magazines, cooking shows, food specialty stores—they're everywhere. Food can be comforting, it can be satisfying, it can be memorable. So, you may eat a carton of ice cream after you get dumped, or you may diet to make sure you fit into your prom dress. This is definitely not healthy, but it may in some strange way be a reasonable response in an unreasonable world.

"That whole slim issue—I hate the media for creating that image. I've had three or four friends who are anorexic, which is not a good thing. My friend was starving—the only thing she ate for one day was chopped-up tomatoes." Alice, 15

So, when does a bad eating habit become an eating disorder? And what is the difference? The following chart helps to clarify the difference between disordered eating and an eating disorder.

	DISORDERED EATING	EATING DISORDER
What it is	A reaction to life situations—a habit.	An illness
What you might be thinking/ doing	Occasional thoughts and behaviors related to your body, foods, and eating that do not lead to health, social, school, and work problems.	Frequent and persistent thoughts and behaviors related to your body, foods, and eating that do lead to health, social, school, and work problems.
How it might affect you	May lead to occasional weight changes or nutritional problems; rarely causes major medical complications.	Can result in major medical complications that lead to hospitalization or even death.
Kinds of help you may need	Education and/or a self-help group can help you to change your eating habits and negative thoughts about your body. Therapy and/or counseling can be helpful but are not usually necessary. Problem may go away without treatment.	Specific professional medical and mental health treatment is required. Problem does not go away without treatment.

THE LINK BETWEEN EATING DISORDERS AND DEPRESSION

Although a lot of research has been done on eating disorders, there is still no simple answer as to why some people suffer from them while others do not. If it was just about the media images of thinness and beauty we are bombarded with, then we would all have food issues. If it was only about traumatic life events, then every child whose parents divorced would be anorexic. It's just not that simple.

"It's very hard to look back and see what caused my eating disorder or my depression. I think part of it is genetic and part of it was situational, as in a bunch of things were happening at the same time and I wasn't dealing with them. I wasn't talking to anyone. I didn't really have a lot of support. I'm on Prozac now. That's the main drug I've been on since I was 16, but since going to university and with the eating disorder under control, I've still dealt with a lot of depression. I still think it's all related, though. I'm happy that food is no longer an addiction or whatever, but it never really totally goes away because I still struggle with depression from time to time. It's hard." Heather, 23

It is known that adolescents who suffer from depression and anxiety are at greater risk of developing an eating disorder. This does not mean that if you are depressed or anxious, you will automatically develop an eating disorder. It just means that since your chances are statistically greater, you need to watch out. This also means that if you have a friend who you think is depressed, you might also want to keep an eye on their eating behavior. This can be a little tricky, because depression can mess with your appetite, often making you want to eat less—but this is not the same as an eating disorder. So don't jump to any immediate conclusions; it's just something else to consider.

FOODS THAT CAN AFFECT YOUR MOOD

Sugars and carbohydrates raise serotonin levels by increasing the absorption of tryptophan in the brain. Low levels of serotonin have been linked to depression. So, those low-carb, low-sugar diets may actually be bad for your mood.

FISH CAN MAKE YOU HAPPY.

It is believed that people who live in the Mediterranean have less depression than North Americans because they eat so much fish, which is high in omega-3 fatty acids. There is evidence that a diet high in omega-3 fatty acids has a positive impact on your mood.

Caffeine drains energy and stimulates anxiety. Alcohol is equally hard on your body. Some people believe that depression is actually your body's response to you abusing it—it's telling you to give it a break.

WAY BEYOND A HABIT: EATING DISORDERS

"An eating disorder is not a diet, a sign of personal weakness, or a problem that will go away by itself. An eating disorder requires professional attention."
— Harvard Eating Disorders Center

Disordered eating is behavior that is almost expected in adolescents, but an eating disorder is an illness which can be life-threatening. So, it's one thing to have lousy eating habits, but it's another thing altogether to have an eating disorder. When you are depressed, poor eating habits are often related to a loss of appetite as a result of the illness. An eating disorder, on the other hand, is not about food at all; it's more about control. In many ways, an eating disorder is a coping strategy used by someone to get through a tough time. If your life seems out of control, being able to control one aspect of it (what you take into your body) can make you feel more secure. Although there is a big difference between disordered eating and an eating disorder, it's important to know that the habits and thoughts of someone who has disordered eating can be leading towards an eating disorder.

Two of the most common eating disorders are **anorexia nervosa** and **bulimia nervosa**. These are both very serious and sometimes fatal disorders.

CHECK IT OUT
page 154

"Eating disorders have the highest mortality rate of any mental illness." — www.sheenasplace.org

Anorexia Nervosa

People who suffer from anorexia deprive themselves of food (starve themselves).

People suffering from anorexia:
◆ refuse to maintain a body weight that is at or above a minimally normal weight for their age and height.
◆ have an intense fear of gaining weight or becoming fat, even though they are underweight.
◆ have a disturbed perception of their body weight and/or shape, place an undue emphasis on their body weight or shape according to their own self-evaluation, or deny the seriousness of their low body weight.

Bulimia Nervosa

People who suffer from bulimia overeat and then purge (make themselves throw up or take laxatives).

People suffering from bulimia:

◆ have episodes of binge eating (rapid consumption of a large amount of food in a short period of time).

◆ experience a feeling of lack of control over their eating behavior.

◆ make themselves vomit/throw up.

◆ use laxatives and diuretics (substances that remove water from the body).

◆ diet, fast, or engage in strict exercise programs to avoid gaining weight.

◆ are overly concerned with their body shape and weight.

There is a third type of eating disorder that is less well known, called **binge eating disorder**. Someone who suffers from this (also known as **compulsive overeating**) overeats impulsively and uncontrollably. They do not make themselves throw up, but they may diet or fast after the fact.

"I think it's pretty common for bulimic people to be embarrassed about it, more so than if they are anorexic, because in our society having restraint and being able to resist food is [seen as] a good thing. People are applauded for it, whereas if you are into throwing up, that's a little weird. I don't think any eating disorder should be considered okay." Heather, 23

CAUSES OF AN EATING DISORDER

People who suffer from eating disorders have negative images about their bodies and themselves. They often find that controlling their body helps them to feel more in control of their life. An eating disorder is rarely about food, it's about how people feel about themselves. Food is just a tool that is used for self-expression. As mentioned earlier, people with eating disorders often struggle with anxiety, depression, and loneliness.

"I think that my eating disorder was probably an attention-getter, because I remember a lot of people knew about it. I'm a firm believer that if someone is doing something for attention, you need to give them some attention, but in a positive way. I would get a lot of, 'You're just doing that for attention,' but there was so much more behind it. It wasn't a 'look at me,' it was a 'help me.' It was just something to say that something was wrong." Marlee, 21

"I think that somewhere I was maybe partially concerned about my appearance, but I don't think that was the catalyst for what went on. I think it was a lot more about control." Heather, 23

There is some evidence that eating disorders are linked to genetics. If one of your parents or another close relative has struggled with an eating disorder, your risk of having one yourself is greater. Living in our beauty-obsessed society can also make it hard to feel good about yourself. If your body doesn't measure up to the "ideal," it's hard not to feel a little out of control. And it's not just girls who suffer from eating disorders: between 10 and 15 percent of people who are diagnosed with bulimia nervosa are boys and men. Boys who participate in sports where they need to meet specific weight requirements, such as wrestling, are more likely to struggle with eating disorders.

"An American study conducted in 1992 revealed that 40 percent of fourth-graders diet either 'very often' or 'sometimes.'" — Harvard Eating Disorders Center

TRIGGERS

For someone who struggles with an eating disorder, there may be certain things that can trigger an episode of bingeing or not eating. It is important to get involved with a support group or one-to-one counseling to help yourself identify what those things might be. As with depression and many other mood disorders affecting adolescents, some common triggers for eating disorders include traumatic life events (the death of a loved one, the end of a relationship) and transitions (change of schools, moving). Anything which can make you feel that your life is out of control can potentially launch you back into unhealthy behaviors as you attempt to regain control. Get to know your triggers so you can look out for them and get the support you need when things are looking rough.

TREATMENTS

It's important to get help before serious damage is done. Starvation can damage your heart and affect your blood pressure. Purging (throwing up and taking laxatives) can damage your gastrointestinal tract and your esophagus. Binge eating can lead to diabetes.

"Fifteen percent of people who develop anorexia die either directly from the disease or from consequences of it, such as heart failure."
— www.sheenasplace.org

People who suffer from an eating disorder usually have to deal with their disease all their life. There is no pill to make them better, although antidepressants can alleviate some of the symptoms of depression and anxiety that tend to make eating disorders worse. An eating disorder requires treatment—you can't fix it on your own. There are many treatment centers and programs for people with eating disorders that can help them to better understand themselves and what they are going through. It's important to remember that *you can get better.*

page 154

PHYSICAL CONSEQUENCES OF WEIGHT LOSS (ANOREXIA)

◆ Difficulty concentrating or thinking clearly
◆ Sensitivity to cold
◆ Lowered blood pressure, which may result in fainting or dizziness
◆ General weakness
◆ Shrinking of muscles and other organs, including the brain
◆ Thinning of hair or hair loss
◆ Pale skin tone (anemic), downy hair (lanugo) on face and arms
◆ Dehydration, which may result in constipation and dry, cracked skin
◆ Osteoporosis (weakening of the bones)
◆ Loss of menstruation (amenorrhea)
◆ Heart failure, death

DIFFICULTY CONCENTRATING.

PHYSICAL CONSEQUENCES OF BULIMIA

◆ Electrolyte imbalance, with possible cardiac and kidney dysfunction as a result of purging (vomiting, laxatives)
◆ Difficulty concentrating on tasks, mood swings due to chemical imbalance
◆ Swollen glands, puffiness in the cheeks, or broken blood vessels under the eyes
◆ Unexplained tooth decay and gum problems
◆ Scarring or red abrasions on top of hands or knuckles
◆ Chest pain, muscle cramps, fatigue

SUSPICIOUS BEHAVIORS

There are some particular behaviors associated with anorexia and bulimia that may be a sign that someone is suffering from an eating disorder. If you think your friend or sibling might be exhibiting some of these behaviors, you should talk to them and encourage them to get help. Don't be surprised if they deny anything is wrong; they may not be ready to acknowledge the problem. They may also just have really bad eating habits—in which case they could still use some help. You may want to talk to an adult about what you think is going on if you feel that it's too much for you to handle. If you think you might have an eating disorder, you need to get help right away. An eating disorder will not go away on its own.

Behaviors Associated with Anorexia

- Dieting, eating fewer calories, only "safe" foods (low or no fat)
- Hoarding, concealing, picking at, crumbling, or throwing away food
- Engaging in compulsive or ritualistic behavior, such as cutting food into small pieces or rearranging food
- Preoccupation with food, reading recipes, preparing food only for others, measuring and weighing food

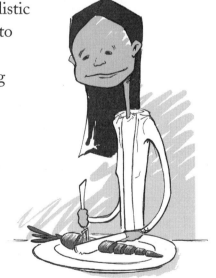

- Wearing baggy or layered clothing to conceal weight loss or to keep warm
- Engaging in compulsive activity and excessive exercise
- Social withdrawal, secretiveness

Behaviors Associated with Bulimia

- ◆ Preoccupation with and constant concern about food and/or weight
- ◆ Severe self-criticism
- ◆ Self-worth determined by weight
- ◆ Frequent bathroom visits after meals
- ◆ Restricting food when eating in public
- ◆ Impulsivity (with alcohol, spending, decision making, relationships)

GET HELP

There are lots of great resources listed in the **Check It Out section** (on pages 154–55) that can help you to understand eating disorders and that can provide you with ideas on how to help someone who is struggling with one. Just remember that an eating disorder can take a long time to get under control; you need to be patient. For more information on treatment options, see chapter 10.

"You have to sort of be able to put yourself in the sick person's shoes and understand that it isn't a choice for them to have an eating disorder or to be depressed. I didn't want to be a crappy friend or a bad daughter or be unable to go out with my friends. I missed out on what everybody else experienced from 15 to 19 years old. It's helpful if friends can understand that. Be supportive and stand by them as they are. Let them know you know they are struggling and you're there for them." Heather, 23

Chapter 7
Self-Mutilation: Releasing the Pain

For some people, the emotional pain of their life is too much to take. They become numb and overwhelmed by what they are feeling. They can't talk about how they feel, and this makes it even harder to bear. Sometimes cutting or hurting themselves in other ways is how they deal with their depression or other emotional trauma—it's the only way they can express how bad they truly feel. This chapter explores the issue of self-mutilation and how it can impact the life of someone who is depressed.

Claire's father suffers from depression, so she has lived with it her whole life and knows it well. She thinks her depression started in about grade 4. At the time, she ignored it because she didn't really know what it was—she just felt as if she had lost something. She changed schools after grade 6 and had a hard time leaving all the friends she had been with since kindergarten. Being scared of growing up and having things change really caught her.

By the time she was in grade 7, Claire was severely depressed. She started cutting herself, but hid her depression from her friends and family. She finally realized that she couldn't continue putting so much energy into pretending she was happy and that everything was okay. Her parents found out she was cutting herself and took her to see a psychiatrist. "They made me realize something was really wrong. I had just thought that was the way I was, because I had been like that for so long. I was used to it. It was a really long time—three whole years of just being blah." Talking about her feelings was hard for Claire, and although she is still seeing the same counselor, she doesn't really like going.

Cutting was a release for Claire. Sometimes she would skip class and go to the corner store to buy razor blades so she could cut in the school bathroom. Sometimes her need to cut was so great it felt like an emergency—she had to do it.

Claire's psychiatrist prescribed antidepressants, and that helped a lot—it kind of filled in the hole she had been feeling. It has taken her a while to find the right balance of dose and medication. She still has triggers—the change of seasons, for example—that can spark a depression in her. But she pays attention to this and knows that the cold winter months are going to be tough.

When she's depressed, she gets really withdrawn. She stops going to school, stops calling her friends, and basically stops talking. This can be hard, because she knows she has to talk about how she feels in order to get better. But Claire is doing well now. She has a boyfriend, she's doing better in school, she's not cutting, and she is usually able to talk about her emotions. She feels good, but says, "Depression is something you don't get rid of. It's not going to suddenly not be there. It can definitely come back when you least expect it."

You may know people who hurt themselves or you may have noticed unusual scars on a friend's arms or legs. You may have heard other kids talking about cutting or burning. These self-harming behaviors are called **self-mutilation**. This can be a scary and confusing issue both for the people who hurt themselves and for their friends and family.

"It was sort of scary to see the cuts. She really wasn't joking."
Alice, 15

"Cutting is one of those things that, a lot of times, people think you're crazy if you do it, but it's a form of releasing stress." Clifford, 18

UNDERSTANDING SELF-MUTILATION

Many people think that self-mutilation is a way of trying to kill yourself. It often isn't. Self-mutilation is a way of expressing the anger, agitation, and  pain that many people face when they are depressed or suffering from other **page 155** mental health issues.

"Just as depression can be described as anguish turned inward, self-mutilation can be described as psychic pain turned inward in the most physical way. Girls who are in pain deal with that by harming themselves." — Mary Pipher, *Reviving Ophelia*

Sometimes, if people are depressed, it can be hard for them to explain to others how they feel, and they may not even have the energy to try. That isolation can lead them to take their pain and anger out on themselves. They may use a brief episode of self-mutilation as a way to express how they feel. They may scratch up their arms or legs once or twice and then leave it at that. For others, though, it can turn into a regular thing.

"I had thoughts about suicide, but I wouldn't ever have attempted it. [Cutting] was just a way of doing something a lot less severe and a lot less permanent to express what I was feeling. I guess I didn't have any other way. It really scared me, because I was making myself bleed and it freaked me out. I felt that I just had so much pain inside

me and so much I was going through that I felt like nobody could see, so I quantified it. That was what it was about for me, I think. It was like, 'This is how bad it is.'" Marlee, 21

People who cut regularly when they are experiencing severe emotional pain often have a ritual around their cutting that includes a special place and particular tools. The physical pain of self-mutilation replaces the emotional pain they are feeling—it becomes a necessary release. Cutting, burning, scarring (picking at scabs repeatedly to make a deeper scar), and pulling out your hair are all types of self-mutilation. Some people bang their head until they pass out, or break their own bones. Self-mutilation is not about wanting to die, it's about trying to feel alive. The description of cutting as "a bright red scream" really illustrates what it's about.

"Cutting was because I needed to get back into my life. You sink into this place where you can't think or feel, you don't know what you're doing. My brain, subconsciously, would tell me that's what I had to do to get out of the horrible hell I would snap into. Cutting yourself is pain and blood and living, and it's taking away the pain of being this empty person." Claire, 17

When a person's pain or depression is very intense, they may become disconnected from their real self (known as a **dissociative state**) in order to protect themselves from their feelings. They feel so numb and lost that it's as if they are floating above the rest of the world or becoming part of the furniture or drifting away entirely. The physical pain of self-mutilation can snap them back into the real world.

"When I cut myself, it was almost like blacking out. Something would snap in my mind." Claire, 17

THE IMPACT OF SELF-MUTILATION

While self-mutilation can be a real release for the people who do it, it can also be quite scary for them. Once the act of cutting and the release of blood have revived them, they can be quite frightened by what they have done to themselves.

"It wasn't the perfect solution, of course, because after you cut yourself you think: 'I'm totally crazy. I'm going completely crazy.' Then you're freaked out, sometimes more than you were in the beginning, but it's continual because, once you get into that place ... you can't talk to people, you can't think, you can hardly move around ... That's why I thought I had to do it or else I'd die. There are other things you can do, but all I could see was that I had to cut myself. Cutting, for me, wasn't something avoidable." Claire, 17

Many people who self-mutilate do not feel any pain when they are hurting themselves. They can break their own bones, burn themselves with hot irons, or cut up their arms—with no feeling of pain. Researchers have discovered that, for some people, the stress of traumatic memories or emotional pain causes the brain to release chemicals that act as a kind of pain reliever. These chemicals are powerful opiates that block the physical pain of self-mutilation. Some researchers believe that cutting and other self-harming behaviors can become addictive as a person begins to crave that rush of opiates and the calming effect they have come to rely on. So, once someone starts cutting, it can be hard to stop, even if they know that it's not a healthy thing to do.

There can also be a lot of shame involved in self-mutilation. Although you may be attached to your scars and the way in which they comfort you, you may feel afraid that somebody could find out about them. In this way, self-mutilation is a lot like an eating disorder: it forces you to live a secret life. If you have cut up your arms, you will probably wear long-sleeved shirts to cover your scars. If you are anorexic, you will probably wear long, baggy clothing to cover your disappearing body. The difference is, once you have recovered from an eating disorder, your body will plump up and you will reveal the new, healthy you. Once you have stopped cutting, your scars will still be there—and this can make it hard to move forward. However, there are ways to minimize the scars of self-mutilation. Plastic surgery can be very effective, and can help in the recovery process.

COMMON TRIGGERS FOR SELF-MUTILATION ◄ • • • • •

There are some common triggers for adolescents who self-harm. These include:

memories

◆ memories of sexual or
  physical abuse
◆ traumatic life events
  (death or illness)
◆ overwhelming feelings
  of sadness and
  depression

BODY MODIFICATION AS SELF-MUTILATION?

Body modification is the act of physically altering your body, and it is done around the world for religious, cultural, and social reasons. Today, there is a lot of controversy about body modification because some people believe it is a form of self-mutilation. Are breast implants self-mutilation? How is cutting or scarring yourself to express your personal sense of pain any different from having bags of liquid surgically implanted in your breasts in reaction to your dissatisfaction with your body? It all comes down to our perceptions of "normal," and in our beauty-obsessed culture the messages can be pretty confusing.

A person's relationship with their body can be complex, and, as with eating disorders, it is sometimes the vehicle through which they can control an otherwise chaotic life. If someone is experiencing intense emotional pain, they may control that pain by self-mutilating. If someone is experiencing social isolation and personal anguish as a result of their dissatisfaction with their body, they may try to control that pain through body modification.

BODY MODIFICATION THROUGHOUT HISTORY ◄• • • •

People have been altering their bodies for centuries in attempts to please their gods, gain respect from their peers, and conform to images of beauty.

Aztec priests pierced their cheeks and lips, slashed their tongues, spilled their blood, and sometimes castrated themselves to honor their gods.

Mayan Indians (both male and female) tattooed their entire bodies, and pierced their noses, ears, lips, navels, tongues, and genitals. They also shaped their babies' foreheads with wooden molds and crossed their eyes (permanently) by dangling a ball between them. These things were all done in the name of beauty.

The Chinese practice of foot binding was only outlawed in 1930. Before this time, girls as young as six were taught to bind their feet so that the bones would be pushed downward and their toes would curl up underneath their feet. They thought this made their feet look like lotus flowers, considered a symbol of beauty and eroticism.

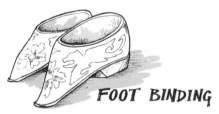

FOOT BINDING

Throughout the world today, people modify their bodies for religious reasons (male circumcision) or social reasons (facelift). Reality makeover shows present these social acts of body modification as "normal" and acceptable. People who loathe their bodies enough to risk their health (and even their lives) in order to shape themselves into something more "acceptable" may not be that far off in their thinking from people who cut their bodies to release their emotional pain.

THE LINK BETWEEN SELF-MUTILATION AND DEPRESSION

It is not surprising for many people that there is a link between self-mutilation and depression. In many ways, self-mutilation is the ultimate expression of depression as anger turned inwards. It is an extreme measure taken to relieve extreme pain. Researchers who have studied bipolar disorder in young women have found that it is not uncommon for girls to self-mutilate as they try to relieve the severe agitation that is often a part of the disorder. For them, self-mutilation provides relief from emotional despair. It has also been reported that many young girls who self-mutilate have experienced significant trauma, such as childhood sexual abuse. Painful memories of destructive experiences can trigger the need to self-mutilate. Research also indicates that a significant number of people who cut also suffer from eating disorders, primarily bulimia.

This does not mean that if you have bipolar disorder, have experienced a significant trauma, or are struggling with an eating disorder, you will inevitably self-mutilate. These are just statistics that clarify for the rest of the world who self-harms and perhaps why they do it.

GET HELP

It is very important to get help if you feel like hurting yourself in any way. There are safer and healthier ways to handle the pain and agitation of your depression. If you are already cutting or know someone who is, you need to find someone to talk to. It is important to try to share your feelings with someone. Start slowly. Find someone you trust, someone you think might understand. And don't be discouraged if the first person you approach turns out to be the wrong choice; sometimes it takes a few tries before you find the person who is going to be willing and able to help you. For more information on treatment options, see chapter 10.

Chapter 8
Depression and Gender:
The Differences between Boys and Girls

The differences between boys and girls may seem obvious to you, but apart from the biology of it all, it can get a little confusing. For this reason, scientists, doctors, parents, and many others have been studying the social and emotional differences between the two sexes for generations. This chapter explores these differences and looks at the different ways boys and girls are affected by and respond to depression.

When Victor was six years old, his mother moved to Canada and left him behind to live with his grandparents in his home country. He missed his mother a lot, but he eventually adjusted to his new life without her. He became very close to his grandparents and regarded them as his parents. Victor never knew his father. It was difficult to see other kids with their parents at school events or other places—it made Victor feel different and lonely. When he was 16, Victor's mother returned and moved him to Canada, where she had established her new life. Adjusting to a new country, a new language, and a new relationship with his mother was really hard for Victor.

In Canada, Victor started to get into trouble. He felt angry and depressed, and didn't know how to express what he was feeling. For the first two weeks in his new school he didn't speak to anyone. He eventually made friends, but would often get into physical fights and has even been in trouble with the law. He finds the pressures of school and trying to figure out what he wants to do with his life sometimes overwhelming.

Victor's mom has been supportive and has encouraged him to go to anger management classes. Even though he still gets depressed and angry, Victor has learned a lot about himself and now knows when to walk away from a situation where he might lose his cool. Victor says, "My depression is UGLY! It's worse than what the devil would look like, especially when I'm really angry and can't hold it anymore. I'm at the limit, just ready to spill it out. If I don't go to the gym or play ball and there's someone in front of me that says something wrong, it triggers the whole thing and it gets bad."

Taking some space and time for himself helps Victor when he's angry. In his anger management class he has learned how to use deep breathing to calm himself down. Victor still has moments when things get hard, but he's finally looking forward to his future. He hopes to finish high school in the next year and plans to go to college.

Sugar and spice and everything nice—frogs and snails and puppy dog tails. These descriptions couldn't be more different, and although it's an old saying, in many ways it still holds true. Or at least our society still nurtures boys and girls as if it were true. A lot of progress may have been made since your parents were teenagers. We may be more open to talking about how we feel, and gender roles may have become blurred as men and women share family responsibilities more and more equally; but the emotional and social differences between boys and girls are still there—because it's not only about nurture, it's also about nature.

CHECK IT OUT

page 156

A COMBINATION OF BIOLOGY (NATURE) AND SOCIETY (NURTURE)

Finding boys to interview for this book was a challenge. It's not as if there aren't any depressed boys out there, but they seem more reluctant to talk about it. In many cases they don't even recognize depression when they are feeling it. Girls, on the other

hand, were more than willing to speak about their experiences and to share their stories. They had great insights into the time frame of their depression, how it made them feel, how it affected their relationships with other people, and how they are dealing with it. So what makes boys and girls so different when it comes to dealing with their own mental health?

"Guys can cry too, even though they don't like to, but they're more afraid to show their emotions in case people think they're weak. Sooner or later, though, you will show your emotions in public, not just anger. Guys don't really talk to their friends. It's really hard for them to find someone they can trust." Victor, 18

The reported rates of depression for boys and girls are interesting. Research shows that in childhood, depression is slightly more common in boys than in girls. In adolescence, the rates of depression are much higher in girls. It's important to remember, though, that rates of depression are based on what is reported to researchers—it is hard to report something that hasn't been identified.

Some people believe that the reported rates of adolescent depression are inaccurate because so many cases are not identified. They believe that how we socialize our children masks what is really going on. They suggest that in young children, girls are overlooked in the statistics because they are socialized to be quiet and unassuming. Boys are expected to be outgoing and get into trouble, and when they do, they get the help and attention they need (and show up more in the rates of depression). Meanwhile, the girls often remain quietly ignored.

In adolescence, this all changes as girls become more outspoken and in tune with their emotions, or at least willing to talk about them. Boys tend to become more withdrawn at this age and less communicative—their depression now going unnoticed and even unidentified within themselves (and so they disappear from the rates of depression).

Research has shown that there are two important biological differences between boys and girls that can affect their behavior. Firstly, girls are more verbal than boys; girls talk earlier and more fluently than boys. Boys eventually catch up, but girls get a head start in this department. Secondly, boys tend to be more physically active than girls. This means that they are often more visible than girls as they express themselves through physical action.

For adolescent boys, their biological tendency to express themselves physically instead of verbally may actually hide their depression. Their aggressive behavior makes sense in relation to our traditional expectations of masculinity, whereas the traditional view of the depressed person is that he is sad and lethargic. This means that when a boy acts out aggressively, it is often blown off as "boys will be boys"—expected and even socially accepted behavior. It is often not until a boy has got into serious trouble with the law or is having major difficulties at home or in school that depression is even considered.

"There's a common stereotype: guys are supposed to be rough and tough, girls are supposed to be these soft little weaklings who cry and stuff like that. That's the main reason it keeps going on—it's because of the stereotype. As you're growing up, you're supposed to be a certain way. When you're raised a certain

STEREOTYPES

TOUGH GUYS AND GIRLY GIRLS

way, girls are more willing to talk about their problems and guys are not. Guys don't usually talk about their problems. They're always kept inside. Girls, most of the time, can talk to their mothers or things like that. Guys can't usually talk to their fathers." Clifford, 18

A GIRL'S WORLD

It would be irresponsible for us to ignore the statistics, even if we are not convinced they are true. So, in line with the belief that adolescent girls actually do experience depression more than boys, there are some interesting thoughts about why this might be.

As discussed earlier, some people believe that it has to do with the way girls are socialized. Girls tend to put more value on their personal relationships, and when those go bad, they are deeply affected. Girls also tend to blame themselves when things go wrong, whereas boys don't take things so personally. These traits put girls at higher risk of becoming depressed because they are more likely to internalize their anger and have negative thoughts about themselves.

There is also some thought that there might be a connection between female hormones and depression. Before puberty, the rates of depression are fairly equal between boys and girls (as mentioned before, the rate of depression is slightly higher in boys). Once puberty hits, the rates almost double for girls. Related to this, people have also noticed that as the age of puberty decreases (girls are getting their periods and going through puberty much earlier than in previous generations), the rates of depression in adolescents are increasing. This means that girls are developing both their bodies and their depression at younger ages than in previous generations.

SEROTONIN AND GENDER

As described in chapter 2, serotonin is a hormone which we all have that affects our moods. It has been discovered that women synthesize serotonin 50 percent slower than men. This may account, in part, for the higher rates of depression in adolescent girls and women. A man may have extra protection against depression because he naturally has higher levels of serotonin in his brain.

Here are some other things that might put girls at higher risk of getting depressed:

Body changes: When boys go through puberty, they become muscular and grow taller. When girls go through puberty, their bodies become curvy and they develop more body fat. They lose that skinny little girl they once knew—the one who looked so much like the models in all the magazines. A girl's perception of herself in a world that values thinness as beauty may become negative if she doesn't meet those social standards.

Independence: Many parents tend to let their sons have more independence than their daughters, and because of this, boys may be more willing to take risks and be more experienced at handling the world around them. Girls often don't have this experience, so venturing out into the world can be more stressful for them.

Sexual abuse: Girls are more likely to be victims of sexual abuse, and the fear of this happening can be really intimidating for any young woman. This can impact how a girl views the world and may make her feel insecure.

FEAR

The way girls are socialized may make them susceptible to depression, but those same qualities may also make their recovery easier. Being able to acknowledge and talk about how you feel can make dealing with it a lot easier. Boys often feel they have to handle their depression themselves in order to be the "strong" men that the world expects them to be.

"I think it's definitely way easier to be depressed if you're a girl than a guy, because to become not depressed is by realizing that you are depressed. That's the only way you'll be able to change things in your life. Guys, though, are discouraged from talking about their feelings and all that. They don't want to talk about it. They don't even know they're depressed." Susan, 19

A BOY'S TAKE ON IT

Adolescent girls and boys approach life in their own particular ways. Here are some of the things that boys are more likely to engage in when they are dealing with depression or other mood disorders:

Substance Use

There is a definite relationship between substance use and depression. The initial buzz you get when you drink may reduce your anxiety or lift your depression

DRINKING

for a while, but some people report that they have actually become depressed *after* using drugs and alcohol. Some people who use drugs and alcohol regularly and excessively may in fact be using those substances to hurt themselves intentionally.

SOME PEOPLE USE SUBSTANCES TO HURT THEMSELVES INTENTIONALLY.

"I smoke a little weed, I get hungry, eat a bit, and my high is gone in a couple of hours. After that, you're dealing with the exact same thing you were dealing with before smoking, plus you've wasted more time, so you're actually dealing with more stress. That's why I don't look at drugs as an antidepressant." Clifford, 18

In the U.S., boys are more likely than girls to use hard drugs (including heroin, crack, cocaine, LSD, and inhalants). If you are high or drunk, you may take part in things that could endanger your life and the lives of others, such as reckless driving. Under the age of 18, boys are 10 times more likely than girls to be arrested for a drug- or alcohol-related offense.

CHECK IT OUT
page 156

Violence and Aggression

In boys, depression tends to present itself as anger, which they often take out on the world around them. This puts them at higher risk of getting into trouble with the law or of getting physically hurt. Boys tend to express their anger and frustrations in a more aggressive way than girls. Again, this has a lot to do with the way in which boys are socialized and the way in which

DEPRESSION TENDS TO PRESENT ITSELF AS ANGER.

our society expects them to behave. It is considered "natural" for girls to talk about their feelings and cry openly, while boys are often viewed as weak if they do the same. While girls are more likely to internalize their feelings of anger and frustration, hurting themselves through cutting or controlling their eating, boys often take those same feelings out on the people and the world around them. In this way, boys' depression can often be overlooked because, instead of seeming sad, they appear angry, edgy, or hostile.

CHECK IT OUT
page 156

"When I'm depressed, I feel mad and I always try to launch my anger and depression towards something else, or someone else in some cases." Victor, 18

"For girls, I think it's physical. They become anorexic, they stop eating, they cut themselves. Guys are different. Some of them don't talk about it. I think guys tend to bottle it up and it comes out in anger or even violence. I think there's a connection between anger and depression." Ernesto, 20

TOUGH GIRL

In the past few years there has been an increase in violence among girls—it's no longer just a boys' issue. Some people say this female aggression is a result of confusion caused by the blurring of gender roles. Perhaps girls feel they have to be more aggressive and less passive as they are released from traditional notions of femininity. Loosely defined gender roles can also be confusing for boys, who may be unsure as to what is expected of them.

Suicide

"I've never harmed myself, but I think about it a lot when I'm depressed. Before, if I'd had a gun or something, I'd probably have just shot myself." Ernesto, 20

In North America, more girls try to kill themselves than boys, but more boys actually die from suicide. This is mostly because boys use methods that are more violent and lethal. Girls tend to take a more passive approach and do things like overdose on pills, which they can often be saved from. This difference between boys and girls in the aggressiveness of suicide attempts is interesting when you consider the cultural factors that play into it. In China, where girls are more likely to have access to lethal pesticides, more girls than boys complete suicide. In North America, our easy access to guns (particularly in the U.S.) has a direct impact on the suicide rate among boys, as this is in many cases the tool that they use. For more information on suicide, see chapter 9.

WARNING

Any thoughts or talk of suicide must be taken seriously. If you are feeling suicidal, you must find someone to talk to *now*. If your friend is talking about suicide, you need to get the help of an adult right away. This is not something you should deal with on your own. Don't keep it to yourself even if your friend has asked you not to tell anyone. Better to have an angry friend than a dead one. Don't keep it a secret!

Chapter 9
Suicide: No Turning Back

Suicide is a scary issue—scary for someone who is thinking about it and also scary for the friends and family of that person. Suicide is a desperate measure, and it's also a permanent one; once it's done, there's no turning back. This chapter looks at the issue of suicide and explores what it means to be suicidal and how it can impact your life and the lives of the people around you. If you or someone you know is talking or thinking about suicide, you need to get help right away.

When April was very young, her parents split up. It was a rough divorce, and her mother eventually moved away with April and her younger brother. April's father had little contact with his children and was frustrated by the situation. Soon, April's mom remarried and had twins with her new husband.

April was often responsible for the care of her younger siblings and got little support from her older sister (from her mother's first marriage). She didn't like her new stepfather and felt unhappy in her family situation. But nobody realized quite how unhappy she was until, at the age of 12, she spent six months living with her dad. One day he came home to find her on the bathroom floor, vomiting. She had skipped school and had taken an overdose of a common brand of pain reliever. As she was throwing up, she apologized for what she had done, saying it was a stupid thing to do. Her father rushed her to the hospital, where she was treated and released the next day. Her family was frustrated that she was released so quickly without anyone finding out why she had tried to hurt herself. No one seemed to provide any support to them.

April returned home to her mother and saw little of her father after that. She did spend some time in the following summers at her grandmother's cottage. People noticed that she seemed a bit withdrawn, spending a lot of time reading and writing in her journal. When she was home with her mother, April's father spoke with her and her brother often on the phone and tried to remain a part of their lives. At this point April was having a hard time at school and was seeing a psychiatrist, who had diagnosed her as having bipolar disorder and had started her on antidepressants. It's possible that the antidepressants intensified her mania and caused her disorder to spiral out of control.

She was hospitalized once because she said she was hearing voices and had threatened to hurt herself. On the day she died, April and her father spoke on the phone twice. She was upset that she had broken up with her boyfriend but otherwise sounded fine. Her friends at school said she seemed happy that day. When her mother came home, she found April's lifeless body—she had hanged herself in the bathroom. April was 15.

Suicide is a confusing and frightening thing. No one really knows why someone would commit suicide. Even if the person leaves a note explaining why they have done it, a suicide always leaves a lot of unanswered questions. Just as there is no one thing that causes depression, there is no one thing that leads directly to suicide. Someone who attempts or completes suicide is trying to escape intense emotional pain. This pain can be caused by many things. Some people believe that the increased access to guns and gun culture in North America are in part responsible for the incidence of adolescent suicide. Others believe that the increase in adolescent depression is responsible for the high rate of adolescent suicide. It's probably safe to say that these are both contributing factors.

SAYING GOODBYE...

▶ SOME FACTS ABOUT SUICIDE IN THE U.S.

Suicide is the third leading cause of death among young people aged 15 to 24. In 2001, 3,971 suicides were reported in this group. Of the total number of suicides among those aged 15 to 24 in 2001, 86 percent were male and 14 percent were female. American Indians and Alaskan Natives have the highest rate of suicide in the 15-to-24 age group. In 2001, firearms were used in 54 percent of youth suicides.

Between 1980 and 1996, the suicide rate for African-American males aged 15 to 19 increased 105 percent. In 1999, 20 percent of American high school students reported having seriously considered or attempted suicide during the previous 12 months. Eight percent of students who seriously considered suicide actually attempted it.

RISK FACTORS IN SUICIDE

Depression is one of the biggest risk factors for suicide. Most youth who attempt or complete suicide are depressed. This does not mean that if you are depressed you are going to be suicidal; it just means that your risk is higher and that you, your family, and your friends need to pay attention to this.

CHECK IT OUT

page 156

"I think the problem with depression and the problem with why people kill themselves or why they go off the edge is because they can't see that, eventually, everything will be fine. That will happen. It's gotta happen. No matter what situation you're in, whether it's going to last two days or two years, it's still worth waiting to see yourself get better." Susan, 19

Some other risk factors for adolescent suicide include:

Other mood disorders: As with depression, if you suffer from a mood disorder such as anxiety disorder or bipolar disorder, your risk for suicide is higher.

Previous suicide attempt: Someone who has attempted suicide before is 100 times more likely to complete suicide than someone who has not tried it before.

HOPELESSNESS

Feelings of hopelessness: Feeling hopeless and having a sense that things will never get better can increase your risk for suicide.

EATING
DISORDERS

Eating disorders: Adolescents with bulimia and anorexia often suffer from depression, and this increases their risk for suicide.

Substance use: As discussed in the previous chapter, substance use can be considered a form of slow suicide. Drinking and taking drugs lowers your inhibitions and can lead you to take life-threatening risks that could end your life.

Psychosis: People who suffer from psychoses, experience hallucinations, and hear voices are at increased risk of hurting themselves, including suicide.

Family history of suicide: Losing a parent or other relative to suicide can be overwhelming for an adolescent. It brings suicide into your life and makes it both a reality and a possibility. This experience increases your risk for suicide. Also, some researchers believe that there is a genetic link to suicide and that this trait can be inherited.

STRESSFUL LIFE EVENTS

Stressful life events: Witnessing violence or surviving a disaster can cause extreme stress that can lead to post-traumatic stress disorder and depression.

Significant losses and separations: Feelings of worthlessness, loneliness, and rejection are often the result of losing someone you love through a death or a family breakup. These feelings can lead to low self-esteem and depression.

Physical or sexual abuse: This kind of betrayal and abuse can permanently damage someone's sense of self. This can lead to self-destructive behavior, including suicide.

Poor academic performance: Doing badly in school can affect your self-esteem and make your future look bleak. These feelings can lead to depression.

Poor peer relationships/social isolation: Feeling that you don't fit in anywhere and that you don't have any close friends can be really isolating. This sense of isolation and loneliness can lead to depression.

Family conflict: Fighting and conflict between parents or caregivers can increase your risk for depression and self-destructive behavior.

Hearing about other suicides: It has been proven that the rates of adolescent suicide rise when another suicide is reported in the media.

Issues surrounding sexual orientation: The struggle to come to terms with your sexuality can be very difficult, especially when you are confronting discrimination and social biases. For an adolescent who is homosexual or bisexual, these stresses can lead to depression and self-destructive behavior.

SOME THINGS THAT CAN TRIGGER ADOLESCENT SUICIDE

◆ Relationship problems (breakups and rejection by friends)
◆ Suspension from school and school failure
◆ Getting into trouble with the law
◆ Humiliation (such as being a victim of bullying)
◆ Pregnancy

HUMILIATION

SIGNS TO LOOK OUT FOR

You may be worried about a friend or sibling who you think might be suicidal. If so, you should pay attention to what this person is saying and doing. There are some common signs that may indicate that a person is at risk of attempting suicide. They include the following:

◆ Statements about being worthless
◆ Statements about being a burden to others
◆ Statements of suicidal intentions
◆ Gradual or sudden loss of interest in many things
◆ Apparent attempts to say goodbye to many people
◆ Talking about death, listening to songs about death, or drawing or writing about death
◆ Reckless use of alcohol or drugs, and risky behavior
◆ Giving away valued possessions

WARNING

Any thoughts or talk of suicide must be taken seriously. If you are feeling suicidal, you must find someone to talk to *now*. If your friend is talking about suicide, you need to get the help of an adult right away. This is not something you should deal with on your own. Don't keep it to yourself even if your friend has asked you not to tell anyone. Better to have an angry friend than a dead one. Don't keep it a secret!

WHAT YOU CAN DO

If someone you know expresses a desire or an intention to commit suicide, you should:

◆ Stay calm.
◆ Take the person seriously and say that you want to help.
◆ Don't leave them.
◆ Remove dangerous things from the surroundings.
◆ Call an adult to help.
◆ Ask questions and really listen.

Do not:

◆ Assume this is a bluff.
◆ Challenge the person to go ahead and try it.
◆ Promise to keep it a secret.
◆ Tell them to try to feel differently.

GET HELP

When you are depressed, life can appear overwhelming. It may seem as if you are alone and that you have no future. This is the depression talking, dragging you down and sucking you in. You need to reach out, even though that can seem excruciatingly difficult at times. There is someone out there who will listen to you and help you. Understanding yourself and your depression can protect you from making decisions that could destroy your life, as well as the lives of the people who love you. Once you know the things that can trigger your depression and suicidal thoughts, you can find ways to tackle them.

Please remember that there is no real formula to depression—it will forever be a complicated thing. If you identify with some of the issues mentioned in this chapter, that does not mean that you are going to kill yourself; it simply means that you should get to know more about what is going on with you. Getting information and support can help you through really tough times. Suicide is permanent, but—though it may not seem like it right now—there are things you can do to make your depression temporary.

page 156

If you or someone you know is feeling suicidal, you need to get help now!
In Canada, you can call the Kids Help Phone:
1-800-668-6868
In the U.S., you can call the Suicide Hotline:
1-800-784-2433

Chapter 10

Treatment Options:
Medications and Therapies

This chapter explores the different kinds of treatment that are available to you. It explains the types of medication that may be prescribed for you and various therapies you might try. It also looks at some alternative therapies that could help you out in your recovery. There are a lot of options out there, and it may take a while to find the one thing or combination of things that works best for you.

"It's a terrible, terrible thing when you feel that there's nothing you can do. Mental illness is kind of sticky that way. It's a profound sense of lost control. For someone who's somewhat of a control freak, like me, it's terrifying. That's why getting help was so important for me, because it gave me a sense of power and it gave me a sense of 'Okay, I'm going to fight this. I'm going to tackle this.'" Susan, 19

The variety of medications and therapies is vast for someone who is depressed, bipolar, or suffering from another mood disorder. Once a diagnosis has been made, your doctor will discuss treatment options with you. This can be really confusing. Try to find out all you can about what is being recommended.

Start reading about depression, anxiety, or bipolar disorder. Find out what they are and learn about other people who have dealt with them. Understanding what you are dealing with will be a big help in your recovery.

GET CURIOUS

"Try to get to know your depression rather than trying to hide from it. Try to turn it into something else. Really try to get to know it so well until you can deal with it, even if it's not going to be great. Definitely dealing with it will make it not so bad." Susan, 19

COUNSELING

Sometimes it can be hard to talk to someone about how you are feeling, because those thoughts and feelings can be so scary, but you really need to do this. Find a friend or an adult whom you can trust. This person can help you to find a professional to talk to, or, if you have a family doctor, you can ask the doctor for a referral.

"It really aggravates me and makes me kind of hysterical, talking about your feelings, because they are so terrible. Hearing them come out of your mouth is kind of devastating." Claire, 17

"Get counseling. If the first counselor you see isn't a good fit for you, get another one, until you find someone who is a good fit for you. Most likely, there is someone who is a good fit. For me, it hasn't gone away, but it has certainly become a lot easier. I used to engage in some self-harming behavior and eating disorder stuff, and now I'm way, way far away from that stuff. I'm miles and miles better than I was. I think it's harder when you're a teenager, because you're going through so many other things that inevitably, I think, get better when you get older. I hope that keeps being true." Marlee, 22

Counseling is the word people often use to describe the act of listening to and advising someone. You might also hear people refer to counseling as **talk therapy**, **psychotherapy**, or **supportive counseling**. Through counseling, you can learn how to tackle the stresses in your life and develop a resilience against your depression.

Choosing a Counselor

Your first visit with a doctor or counselor can be a bit frightening, but knowing what to expect can make it easier. There are different kinds of professionals you might go to, depending on who recommends them and what you can afford. Some of them will be accredited (which means they are regulated by a specific professional organization) while others may not be. The fact that someone is a member of a professional organization does not mean this person will be the best choice for you. A good choice includes a good fit of personalities and a comfort level that suits you. **page 157** CHECK IT OUT

"Basically, though, I felt they weren't really understanding what I was saying or that I actually physically couldn't get out of bed. They thought I just didn't want to get up. There's a big difference, and they couldn't get it, so I had a bad, bad experience with counselors on the whole." Isabel, 22

The advantage of seeing someone who is accredited by a professional organization is that you know the person is being regulated and that you can contact the organization if something goes wrong. Also, someone who is accredited will have completed a certain amount of education combined with a significant amount of clinical training. This experience may provide the counselor with insights and resources that someone without that background may lack.

Types of Counselors

When you are choosing a counselor, you have quite a few options. The following types of counselors (also known as mental health professionals) are extensively trained and must be accredited in the United States and Canada.

Psychiatrist: When completing a medical degree, a doctor chooses an area to specialize in, which then becomes the focus of their work. A psychiatrist is a doctor who has chosen to specialize in mental health, such as child psychiatry. Psychiatrists can write prescriptions for medication and can also order physical tests, such as blood work.

Family doctor: Some family doctors are trained in psychotherapy and provide counseling. All family doctors can write prescriptions for medication.

Psychologist: A psychologist will have a graduate degree in psychology (Ph.D. or Psy. D.) and will have spent a significant amount of time doing clinical training. Psychologists will often specialize in a specific area, such as child psychology.

Psychiatric nurse: A psychiatric nurse is a registered nurse who has training in psychotherapy and extensive experience working in psychiatrics.

Social worker: To be an accredited social worker, someone must have achieved a graduate degree in social work (M.S.W.) and will have completed a significant amount of clinical training. There are social workers in schools, in community centers, and in private practices.

There are other professionals who can offer invaluable support to you, but they may not be accredited. These include youth workers, pastoral counselors, and school counselors. They may be people you feel more comfortable talking to, and they will most likely be able to hook you up with the resources you need if you require more support than they can offer you. This can be a great place to start.

"The counselor was extremely helpful. She made me realize that I wasn't pathetic, and that there are other people going through this, and that, although it's a big part of your life, it's just an obstacle you have to get over. She made the point of saying that this wouldn't happen just once in my life, that life goes up and down many times and that's what makes it worthwhile, really. You can't really know what happiness is without knowing what sadness is. That was a big part of it." Caroline, 19

Many professionals whose costs are not covered by health insurance will arrange their fees on a sliding scale to accommodate what you can afford— a sort of "pay what you can" approach.

What to Expect

A first visit will pretty much be the same with any of these professionals. They will probably ask you to tell them a bit about yourself, why you are there, and what you hope to get out of the counseling. It can be hard shopping around for the right person, because every time you try someone new, you have to tell your story all over again. Don't give up, though, because once you find that right person, they can become really important in your life for years to come.

This does not mean that you necessarily need counseling for a long time, but once you have made a connection with someone, you may find it comforting to be able to go back and see that person as the occasional crisis pops up in your life and you require a little extra support. It's important to trust your counselor and to believe that they have your best interests at heart. If you do not feel this way, you need to find another professional. You have the right to switch counselors whenever you want to.

TYPES OF THERAPY

Every professional will have a particular approach that they practice. Some of these may involve a long-term commitment, while others may be more short-term. Find out about the different approaches so you can make the best choice for you. Below are descriptions of some of the most common therapies that mental health professionals might offer.

CHECK IT OUT

page 158

Psychotherapy

Psychotherapy is a general term used to describe treatments that involve talking with a mental health professional. There are many different types of psychotherapy, but most focus on clarification (clarifying what your issues are), reassurance (reassuring you that you will get better), interpretation (interpreting your issues to help you better understand yourself), and education (educating you about your illness and how you will get better). How long you remain in therapy will be determined by you and your doctor.

The most common forms of psychotherapy used to treat depression and other mood disorders are **cognitive behavior therapy** and **interpersonal therapy**. Cognitive behavior therapy helps you to change your negative thinking and be more positive about your life. Interpersonal therapy helps you to develop better ways to deal with and interact with people.

DESENSITIZATION

Other Therapies

Desensitization—exposing you to what you are afraid of in low doses over an extended period of time (used to treat anxiety disorders and phobias)

Hypnotherapy—hypnotizing you to uncover the root of your emotional distress (used to treat emotional and psychotic disorders)

Phototherapy (light therapy)—exposing you to intense light to relieve depression (used to treat SAD)

Electroconvulsive Therapy (ECT)—delivering an electric shock to cause a seizure that may alter your brain chemistry (rarely used on adolescents, but may help someone who is not responding to other treatments and who is severely depressed, suicidal, or manic)

Supportive counseling—talking about the problems you may have in interpersonal relationships or other professional and social situations (used to treat anxiety and depression)

Family therapy—helping families to understand and cope with issues related to depression and other mood disorders

Group therapy—bringing together people who are struggling with similar issues, to share experiences and provide support for each other

MEDICATIONS

Once you have been diagnosed with depression or another mood disorder, your doctor or psychiatrist might prescribe some medication to help you in your recovery. You will be asked a series of questions to determine what is the best medication for you. The kind of medication prescribed will depend on what your diagnosis is, the kinds of medication that have worked for any family members with CHECK IT OUT page 158 the same diagnosis, and your medical history.

Taking medication is a scary thing for many people, and the idea of taking a drug that might change who you are can be terrifying.

"I always thought it would change my personality, and I'd rather be depressed than have my personality changed. My personality is who I am. I find medication hasn't changed my personality but that I can cope better with my depression." Ernesto, 20

"Maybe the drug takes the edge off of it, but it doesn't change your life or anything like that." Heather, 23

"When he gets so depressed that he says he wishes he didn't exist, or the self-loathing gets too much, I would like to see him on medication. Then again, if you start a kid who's nine on medication, when do they come off? Do they ever come off?" Lucy, parent

"Don't be afraid of the label of mental illness or be afraid of taking medications. A lot of parents just don't want to give their kids medicine, but God, if your kid had heart problems or diabetes or anything else, you'd want to give them medication if you knew it was going to make them feel better. It's no different if they are depressed." Maria, parent

For some people, taking medication does not have to be a lifelong commitment. For others, it is. This really depends on your personal story. If you are depressed, it can be really difficult to see past that depression. Counseling may help you, but you may not have enough energy to get there.

"Trying to deal with stuff while you're depressed is impossible."
Susan, 19

Sometimes antidepressants can get you over that hump of feeling sad. They can clear the way to your recovery by giving you the energy and hope you need to start talking about how you feel with someone who can help you. You may not need to be on medication for a long time, but antidepressants might be required to get your recovery started.

"So, the combination of getting the right medication and being in a treatment program where they talk and taught him all these wonderful strategies, cognitive behavioral strategies that he can use—he's got this great tool kit of strategies now that he can use ... if he ever has a really hard situation he has to face or if he outgrows the medication, starts to have a relapse or something." Maria, parent

"The medicine helped. My mom was really supportive. I think, though, that it was really the counselor, and time." Caroline, 19

"I think that if you need to go on medication to be able to cope in order to work at issues and acquire proper coping mechanisms, then I think it's good, but it should be focused more that way, as a tool." Marlee, 21

Depression and Anxiety Disorders

Medications to treat depression are better today than ever before. They work more quickly and have fewer side effects. As mentioned in chapter 2, the newest group of antidepressants are called Selective Serotonin Reuptake Inhibitors (SSRIs). SSRIs are considered the best first approach for adolescents because they have a low risk for overdose and few side effects. CHECK IT OUT page 158

●●► POSSIBLE SIDE EFFECTS OF SSRIs

There are some possible side effects with SSRIs, which will vary from person to person. These side effects often do not last very long. They may include fluctuation in weight, interference in sexual functioning (including inability to achieve orgasm in girls and delay in ejaculation in boys), lack of energy, agitation, nausea, skin rash, headache, and slight hand tremors. Some people will not experience any of these while others will experience more. If your side effects are significant, tell your doctor so that your medication can be changed (some may produce worse side effects than others) or your dosage altered (a lower dosage may reduce the side effects).

SIDE EFFECTS

SSRIs

You will probably recognize the brand names of some of the SSRIs that might be prescribed to you: Prozac, Zoloft, Paxil, Luvox, and Celexa. They may also be referred to by their generic names: fluoxetine (Prozac), sertraline (Zoloft), paroxetine (Paxil), fluvoxamine (Luvox), and citalopram (Celexa). Prozac, Zoloft, and Celexa are most often prescribed to treat depression, while Paxil and Luvox are often prescribed to treat a combination of anxiety and depression.

There are other types of drugs that your doctor may prescribe if SSRIs don't work well for you. Sometimes SSRIs need a little boost from another drug that can counteract the side effects or make the SSRI work better. For example, if you are experiencing low energy while you're on an SSRI, your doctor may prescribe a stimulant to lift you up a bit. These drugs are called **augmenters** because they augment (increase) the efficiency of SSRIs. Augmenters can include a variety of drugs (depending on your issue), including Dexedrine and Ritalin.

MAOIs

There is another classification of drugs that can be used to treat depression. They are called monoamineoxidase inhibitors (MAOIs). They also impact the effect of serotonin in the body, but they have not been proven effective in adolescents. In fact, they can be quite dangerous as they can interact with other drugs and foods. Because of their unreliability, they are prescribed only when SSRIs are ruled out, and they must be monitored closely.

Atypical antidepressants

If SSRIs don't work well for you, your doctor might prescribe another group of medications known as atypical antidepressants. These drugs affect a whole bunch of neurotransmitters, not just serotonin. These medications include Serzone, Effexor, and Wellbutrin.

Bipolar Disorder

If you have been diagnosed with bipolar disorder, your doctor will likely prescribe a different kind of medication from the drugs mentioned above. The medications prescribed to you may have an antidepressant component to them, but they will focus more on controlling the mania of bipolar disorder.

Lithium is probably the most common drug prescribed for

adolescents with bipolar disorder. It is not very clear how lithium works, but it seems to slow down the activity of certain pathways within the brain that may cause mania and depression. Early side effects of lithium may include nausea, vomiting, diarrhea, abdominal distress, headache, excessive thirst, and frequent urination. Other side effects may include hand tremors, weight gain, hypothyroidism, and cognitive problems, such as short-term memory problems or feeling zoned out. These side effects can often be stabilized by having your doctor adjust your dosage.

Tegretol and Depakote are two other medications commonly prescribed to treat bipolar disorder. They are both anti-manic and anti-convulsant drugs. Side effects of these drugs can include nausea, sedation, dizziness, drowsiness, headache, rash, and weight gain. It is important to understand that both of these drugs may interact with other medications, so make sure you talk to your doctor before you take anything else.

Other drugs that may be prescribed to treat bipolar disorder are Neurontin, Lamictal, Topamax, Gabitril, and Trileptal.

Bipolar disorder is a complicated illness and it can be challenging to find the treatment that will work for you. There is a lot of good information out there that will explain the medications, their effects, and their risks. 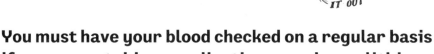 **page 158**

You must have your blood checked on a regular basis if you are taking medications such as lithium, Tegretol, or Depakote. Checking your blood will ensure that your dosage is right (levels of these drugs that are too high can become toxic). Your doctor should arrange for you to have this done.

Don't Stop

As mentioned in chapter 3, it can be hard to get adolescents to take their medication regularly. You are just developing your identity, and taking medication can interfere with your lifestyle and your ideas about who you are. A lot of people say they feel numb or zoned out when they are on medication, and so they may decide to stop taking it.

"For me, because I'm a very emotional person, I thrive on it, even if it's negative. I'd rather feel bad than feel nothing at all, so I went off the medication." Isabel, 22

If you decide you don't like taking your medication or you don't like the way it makes you feel, you need to talk to your doctor about either switching it or reducing your dosage. You should never just stop taking it—that can really mess you up. It can take a while (up to eight weeks) for it to have an effect, but once it's in your system, stopping suddenly can be dangerous. It has been reported that someone who abruptly stops taking lithium after being on it for a while is at an increased risk of attempting suicide. If you suddenly stop taking an SSRI, you may experience withdrawal symptoms including nausea, diarrhea, restlessness, tremors, sleep problems, and nightmares.

"Above all, I don't want to go back on medication. I don't think that's really what I need. I think I just need to realize I'm not as stupid as I think I am, that I can do things." Isabel, 22

No one is thrilled at the idea of taking a pill, but some people notice a definite, positive difference in themselves when they are on medication. They feel more energetic, happier, and calmer.

For them, taking medication is a lot easier than dealing with the instability and weight of their moods.

"I don't care. It's only a pill. It's better than depression." Ella, 12

"Since I'm on antidepressants, I can't sink very low. Antidepressants aren't there to make you feel happy all the time, but they definitely don't let you fall all the way into oblivion. It's almost impossible." Susan, 19

THE LINK BETWEEN TREATMENT AND SUICIDE

There have been some links made between treatment (medication and/or psychotherapy) and an increased risk of suicide. It is not clear what is actually going on, and more studies are being done. One possibility is that people who are severely depressed may lack the energy or motivation to do much of anything, but once they start taking an antidepressant or begin counseling, and it starts to relieve some of the symptoms of their depression, they may notice increases in their energy levels. For someone who is already suicidal, treatment (including antidepressants) can unlock the energy needed to follow through with the desire to commit suicide. It is important to tell your doctor (or any adult you trust) if you are feeling suicidal.

WARNING

Any thoughts or talk of suicide must be taken seriously. If you are feeling suicidal, you must find someone to talk to *now*. If your friend is talking about suicide, you need to get the help of an adult right away. This is not something you should deal with on your own. Don't keep it to yourself even if your friend has asked you not to tell anyone. Better to have an angry friend than a dead one. Don't keep it a secret!

HOSPITALIZATION

Being admitted to hospital for depression or another mood disorder is relatively uncommon, but it is sometimes necessary. This could be because counseling or medication isn't working and you are getting worse; because close monitoring of a new medication is required; or because you or your family/friends feel that you are a danger to yourself or others, and that you can't control your behavior.

Ideally, you will decide you want to go and will be admitted with your consent (that's called **voluntary**). Sometimes, however, a mood disorder can be so severe that you can't tell the difference between what's real and what's not (that's called **psychotic**), and so you may not be able to determine what's best for yourself at that time. In that case, it may be necessary to admit you without your consent (that's called **involuntary**). Remember that your family and friends are not giving up on you—they are trying to do the best thing for you.

Before you are admitted involuntarily, a doctor will fill out a form that allows anyone (such as an ambulance paramedic) to take you to the hospital and keep you there for a limited period of time (probably 72 hours). The doctors on the ward will assess you to make sure you are safe, and as soon as you are, you become "voluntary," which means you can leave whenever you want to.

Most hospitals have floors or wards designed specifically for teenagers. The nurses are specially trained to help make you as comfortable as possible, and usually there are classrooms on site so that you don't fall behind in school. The length of your stay will depend on how quickly the team can help you recover, but an average might be a few days to a few weeks. Everyone works to get you back home as soon as possible. Visits from your parents and friends, and passes to go out, are allowed as soon as you are felt to be safe.

Even though hospitalization may be unfamiliar to you, it does not need to be scary, especially if you remember that everyone is working to get you back "out" as soon as possible. You can expect to have group therapy, one-to-one counseling, family therapy, and medication while you are in the hospital. Recreational stuff—gym, hikes, and outings—is usually part of the program too. Blood tests or X-rays may be ordered to make sure nothing is physically wrong with you.

Often, the hardest part is figuring out what to tell your friends when you're discharged. You can talk to your nurses and doctors, and work with your family, to come up with a plan. Once you are discharged, you will need to keep seeing your doctor to monitor your progress. Remember, this is all about helping you to get better. Being hospitalized doesn't mean you're crazy, it just means you needed some extra attention and support for a while.

ALTERNATIVE THERAPIES

For some of you, the idea of taking medication is just not on. Maybe you believe that, while you may be feeling a bit low, you're not clinically depressed. Depending on your story, alternative therapies might work for you. It's important to know, however, that if you are severely clinically depressed or have bipolar disorder, you are going to need more help than the following alternative therapies can provide. They may prove to be useful strategies in the maintenance of your strong mental health, but a weekly yoga class is not going to help you control the mania of bipolar disorder.

Herbal medicines

There are herbal medicines that some people believe work just as well as prescribed medications. Herbal medicines are not regulated, so their quality and effectiveness can vary. It's important to remember that the pills you get at the health food store can be just as powerful (and can have just as many side effects) as the pills you get at the drugstore.

You shouldn't take any herbal medicines while you're taking prescription medication as they can react badly together. Let your doctor know what you're up to. It's also a good idea to read up on the natural alternatives that are **page 159** available to you.

ST. JOHN'S WORT

SOME HERBAL REMEDIES COMMONLY USED TO TREAT DEPRESSION ARE:

St. John's wort: Side effects may include nausea, allergic reaction, dry mouth, fatigue.

Valerian: Side effects may include frequent urination, nausea, dry mouth, thirst, dizziness, drowsiness.

S-adenosylmethionine (SAMe): Side effects may include nausea, allergic reaction, dry mouth, fatigue.

"There are thousands of alternatives to antidepressants ... I think what to do for your depression is to try a bunch of stuff and see what works and what doesn't work." Claire, 17

Relaxation

We've all heard about the relaxing effects of yoga and meditation. Practicing these can help you to find a calm space in your head where you can escape to when you are feeling low or anxious. The stretching and breathing exercises that are a part of yoga can slow down your heart rate and increase blood and oxygen flow throughout your body. This can be a good thing if you are sad, tired, stressed out, or anxious. Techniques such as deep breathing and visualization can also help you to get through a rough day or calm you down during a panic attack.

Check out your local yoga center or community center. Often they will offer discounts to students or youth. If you're not into joining a group, you can buy (or get from your local library) a book or video that will show you the basics of yoga, meditation, or relaxation techniques. This way you can practice in the privacy of your own home on your own schedule. Consider, though, that if

RELAXATION

page 159

you're feeling depressed, having a place to go where you will be with other people can take your mind off your mood.

Exercise

People who exercise a lot (especially runners) often talk about the natural high they get from it. This is because, as they exercise, their brains release endorphins, a natural chemical that is similar to morphine. Exercise can also make you feel better because it gets your body moving, may make you feel more in control of your life, and will get you out of the house and into the sunlight. If your school sports teams seem a bit too competitive for you, your neighborhood community center will probably offer programs (basketball, swimming, ball hockey, rock climbing) geared to your age group. Again, if the idea of a group doesn't appeal to you, try going out for a walk. Maybe

RUN RUN RUN

you can find a friend who will go with you.

page 159

VITAMIN

Vitamins

As discussed in chapter 6, what you eat can affect your mood. Eating a balanced and healthy diet can help get your moods back on track. There are also some vitamin supplements, especially vitamin B, that are thought to be effective in easing the symptoms of depression. Check with your doctor before you take any vitamin supplement, to make sure you have the right dose and that it will not interact with any medication you are taking. Vitamins can also be expensive, and given that they have not yet been clinically proven to be effective in treating depression, you may want to try going for that walk first.

CHECK IT OUT

page 159

Homeopathy

Homeopathy stimulates your body to heal itself. A homeopath will ask you a long series of questions to find out about your general health, what your health problems are, what kinds of things you eat and drink, and how you lead your life. Once the underlying problem has been identified, a homeopath will prescribe homeopathic medicine that will stimulate your body to recover. The homeopathic approach to healing is different from conventional medicine in that it aims to cure your illness rather than relieve your symptoms. While homeopathy is growing in popularity, it is still fairly controversial and its benefits are not always clear.

A visit to a homeopath, and homeopathic medicines, can be expensive. If you want to try homeopathy, you should consult with your doctor to make sure any homeopathic medicine you take will not interact with medicines you may already be taking.

You can find homeopathic medicines at your health food store, but before taking any of these you should consult with a homeopath to get a clear picture of what it is you need.

page 159

TAKE YOUR TIME

There is no quick fix for depression. Getting better can be a slow process, and you need to make sure that you are focused on it. This can be really hard, since being depressed can mess with your ability to think straight, feel confident, and focus. Once you have friends and family on board to help you, let them know you need them. They need to understand when to push you and when to step back. That's a difficult thing for people to do when they care about you. But if you work together, you can find the best treatment. This could be medication, alternative therapies, counseling, or a combination of all three.

Don't give up when things don't get better right away. A lot of medications can have side effects, and it may take a while before you find the one that works best for you. It may also take a while for you to find a counselor whom you like and feel comfortable with. Remember, you are buying the counselor's services, just as you would buy a pair of shoes, so make sure you have the right fit.

Treatment is about getting better. The more you know about yourself, what your depression looks like, what is causing it, and what treatments will work best for you, the more power you will have to recover. It's important to believe that you will get better—it's only a matter of time. Surrounding yourself with people who believe in you, and having resources that will support you, will make that time go faster.

AFTERWORD

by Dr. Marshall Korenblum, M.D., F.R.C.P.(C), *Psychiatrist-in-Chief at Toronto's Hincks-Dellcrest Centre for Children and Associate Professor in the Department of Psychiatry, Faculty of Medicine, University of Toronto*

Having read this book, you have learned that depression has many different faces. Although each story has certain similarities, every person also has a unique perspective. Whether you're just having trouble coping with normal mood swings, or you have been diagnosed with clinical depression, or you are worried about your sibling or boyfriend/girlfriend, we hope you found information that was useful to you and that you could relate to. The important point is, there is no single approach to depression. Textbooks don't work for everybody. You need to have a plan that works for *you*.

Seeking help sometimes seems impossible. There are many things people say to themselves that keep them from getting help, for example:

◆ "It's not that bad. If I wait long enough, maybe it'll go away on its own." (denial)
◆ "I'm not worth it/nothing will work/I feel too overwhelmed." (pessimism)
◆ "What if my boyfriend/parents find out? They'll think I'm weak/crazy. You have to be crazy to see a therapist!" (shame)
◆ "It's my fault. I should be able to solve this on my own. I obviously have some character flaw. I just need to try harder." (myths or stereotypes about mental illness)
◆ "What? You expect me to open up to some total stranger, who's just going to label me or tell me what I'm doing wrong? Forget it!" (fear of dependency and fear of judgment)

Taking medication can mean different things to different people. You may actually want a "quick fix" to your problem, and so you may ask for pills. Pills can be a symbol of magic relief for either internal pain or environmental chaos. You might think they will let you off the hook ("It's not me, Mom, it's my low serotonin that's making me so cranky!").

There are many reasons why some adolescents don't want to take medications:

- Sometimes they think that medications mean they've been bad, that they're insane, or that they're weak.
- To some, it feels as if something or someone is controlling their mind.
- Sometimes people are concerned that medication will trick them into believing things are getting better when nothing's really changed. They may ask: "If I feel better, is it because of me or the pill?"
- They might be afraid that the medications will change who they are: "The pills will only make me numb. Then who will I be? Some zombie!"
- There is some irony (or perhaps even hypocrisy) in a doctor asking you to stop smoking pot, only to give you another mood-altering substance that just happens to be his/hers.

It is certainly fair for you to ask, "Whose needs are being met, mine or yours?" Don't get help just because someone else is asking you to. But don't deprive yourself of things that will make you feel better just because of stubborn pride or mistaken ideas about what's causing your problem. All teenagers need love, space, friends, traditions, some limits, and adults who care about them. When it comes to clinical depression, it's unlikely you're going to be able to solve it on your own.

You should seek help if:

- your sadness lasts longer than two weeks in a row;
- you have symptoms such as disturbances in your sleep, appetite, energy, concentration, or sex drive, social withdrawal, or preoccupation with death, especially your own; or
- your sadness is interfering with your life (school marks going down, friendships disappearing, family relationships deterior-

ating, physical health declining, or you are getting involved in dangerous things such as drugs or self-mutilation).

A good place to start would be your parents, but if you can't talk to them (or they are the cause of your depression), then a best friend, schoolteacher or guidance counselor, or your family doctor is a reasonable alternative. Seeing your doctor is a good idea because certain medical conditions can mimic depression. The most common ones are anemia, infectious mono, and low thyroid. These should be ruled out before you come to the conclusion that it's depression. They can be easily diagnosed by a simple blood test, and they're all treatable. Once you've determined that you're physically healthy, discuss a referral to a psychiatrist or other mental health professional who is qualified to deal with your problem.

It's important to know that things are not as hopeless as they appear, and that some people do care about you. By asking yourself some of the following questions, you might be able to find some of that hope and realize that you have people ready to help you:

◆ Whom do you admire?
◆ What did you learn from the last painful event you endured?
◆ When did you last help someone else?
◆ When did someone last help you?
◆ What three things can you be thankful for?
◆ Who has been most important to you in establishing your values?
◆ If you were your parent, how would you help you?

You need not get through this alone, and depression (fortunately) is a treatable condition. If you are feeling worthless, helpless, or hopeless, that's the depression talking. With the right kind of help, you won't feel or think this way forever, and you have a very good likelihood of being able to realize your full potential, whatever that may look like.

RESOURCES

You have many options when looking for help. There are hot-lines you can call and websites you can check out. Here are some that will be good places for you to start and to get help right away. Don't forget that you can call 911 if you think you are dealing with an emergency.

You can call any of the numbers below 24/7 and they will listen to your story and connect you with supports in your community. Whatever you tell them will be confidential, and your call will be free. These resources will also be helpful to friends and family members who are looking for advice on how to support someone they care about.

In the U.S. you can call:

National Hopeline Network (Suicide Hotline) 1-800-744-2433

National Suicide Prevention Lifeline 1-800-273-8255

National Runaway Switchboard 1-800-786-2929

National Domestic Violence Hotline 1-800-799-7233

Childhelp USA (Child Abuse Hotline) 1-800-422-4453

National Sexual Assault Hotline 1-800-656-4673

In Canada you can call:

Kids Help Phone 1-800-668-6868

Parent Help Line 1-888-603-9100

HELP IS
AVAILABLE.

If you have access to a computer, certain websites can be very helpful and can link you to other resources. Many of these are listed in the Check It Out section with more detail explaining what they offer. Please explore them safely, and be careful when you check out links to other sites.

www.nami.org	National Alliance for the Mentally Ill
www.nimh.nih.gov	National Institute of Mental Health
www.cmha.ca	Canadian Mental Health Association
www.mooddisorders.on.ca	Mood Disorders Association of Ontario
www.youthnet.on.ca	Youthnet (youth and mental health)
www.sexetc.org	Sex, etc. (youth health issues)
www.outproud.org	The National Coalition for Gay, Lesbian, Bisexual & Transgender Youth
www.stopbullyingnow.hrsa.gov	Stop Bullying Now
www.nmha.org	National Mental Health Association
www.dbsalliance.org	Depression and Bipolar Support Alliance
www.sheenasplace.org	Sheena's Place
www.hedc.org	Harvard Eating Disorders Center
www.safeincanada.ca	Self-Abuse Finally Ends (Canada)
www.safeyouth.org	National Youth Violence Prevention Resource Center
www.catscanada.org	Creating Awareness of Teenage Suicide
www.suicidepreventionlifeline.org	National Suicide Prevention Lifeline

CHECK IT OUT

Here are some books, magazines, videos, and websites that you may want to check out if you want to know more about a particular issue. These resources are organized by chapter and issue, so you can flip back and forth to this section as you read the book. There are lots of resources out there, and I have only listed a few. If a particular resource interests you, check out its bibliography or reference section and this may point you in the direction of yet more information. You can get most of the books and magazines listed here through your local library; you can probably get online there too, if you don't have a computer at home. Happy searching!

CHAPTER ONE
Depression: Then and Now

Depression through the Ages
The Noonday Demon: An Atlas of Depression by Andrew Solomon
This huge book may seem a bit overwhelming, but it is worth checking out. It combines an account of the author's personal struggle with depression with an in-depth look at the history and social context of the illness.

Melancholia and Depression from Hippocratic Times to Modern Times by Stanley W. Jackson
This book describes the history of melancholia and depression in detail, revealing interesting facts about how the illness and the people who suffered from it were treated.

Brain Development
There is a lot of information on brain development as it relates to mental health issues, especially depression. This is a hot topic right now, so what is up-to-date is mostly available in recent books and magazine articles. Here are some good choices:

TIME magazine (Canadian Edition), "What Makes Teens Tick." May 10, 2004
This article explores new discoveries about the teen brain and their impact on treatments for depression and other mood disorders.

Understanding Depression: What We Know and What You Can Do about It by J. Raymond DePaulo, Jr.
This book contains a solid

explanation of what we know today about how the brain works and about how medications work within the brain to treat depression.

The Teen Brain Book: Who & What Are You? by Dale Carlson
This book, written for teenagers, explains how your brain works and how it affects your life, your personality, and your mental health.

Medications

Medications to treat depression and other mood disorders are also a hot topic, especially in relation to adolescents. You will find some interesting thoughts on the controversy in the following sources:

TIME magazine (Canadian Edition), "Medicating Young Minds." January 19, 2004
This article explores the controversy around drug treatment for adolescent mood disorders and behavioral problems.

New York Times Magazine, "The Antidepressant Dilemma." November 21, 2004
This article explores the link between the use of antidepressants and teen suicide, and details one family's tragic experience.

Celebrities

There are lots of celebrities who have struggled with depression and other mental health issues. Here are some resources that you might want to check out:

It Starts Here: A Guide to Mood Disorders for Teens by the Mood Disorders Association of Ontario (MDAO)
This handbook provides a long list of celebrities who have struggled with mood disorders.

Psychology Today, "Celebrity Meltdown" (November/December 1999)
This article lists famous people, past and present, who have struggled with mood disorders.

On the Edge of Darkness: Conversations about Conquering Depression by Kathy Cronkite
This book contains interviews with celebrities who have struggled with depression and other mood disorders.

Touched with Fire: Manic-Depressive Illness and the Artistic Temperament by Kay Redfield Jamison
This book explores the link between bipolar disorder and the artistic temperament.

CHAPTER TWO
Adolescence: Identity and Chaos

Body Changes

There are some very funny and informative resources that will explain to you what your body is going through. Check out:

What's Going on Down There? Answers to Questions Boys Find Hard to Ask by Karen Gravelle
This book is full of information and illustrations about your changing boy body.

What's Happening to Me? A Guide to Puberty by Peter Mayle
A hilarious and fun look at the changes everyone goes through during puberty.

The Period Book: Everything You Don't Want to Ask (But Need to Know) by Karen Gravelle
This book contains lots of information and illustrations about menstruation and your changing girl body.

www.bam.gov
This website is maintained by the Centers for Disease Control and Prevention. It is a very youth-friendly site and explains all sorts of issues related to your physical and emotional health.

www.kidshealth.org
This website has a teen section with lots of information about adolescent health issues and body changes.

www.4girls.gov
Sponsored by the National Women's Health Information Center, the U.S. Department of Health and Human Services, and the Office on Women's Health, this website is full of information on girls' health issues.

Healthy Sexuality

Here are some great resources that will help you to understand your sexuality and will support you in making healthy decisions.

The Little Black Book: A Book on Healthy Sexuality, Written by Grrrls for Grrrls
A great book written by a group of young women in Toronto. To get your hands on a copy of this, contact St. Stephen's Community House in Toronto at 416-925-2103.

www.pflag.org
The website of Parents, Families & Friends of Lesbians & Gays. The site contains lots of information about coming out and getting support from friends and family.

www.outproud.org
Another great site that offers
lots of information and support
to gay, lesbian, bisexual, and
transgender youth.

www.teenwire.com
The website of Planned
Parenthood Federation of
America, containing lots of
youth-friendly information
on healthy sexuality and
related issues.

www.teengrowth.com
This website offers information
on adolescent health issues and
is produced by a group of pedia-
tricians and health professionals.

www.sxetc.org
The website of Sex, Etc., part
of the National Teen-to-Teen
Sexuality Education Project
developed by the Network
for Family Life Education at
Rutgers University. It is
designed for teens by teens,
and has tons of information
on sexual health.

Friends/Peer Groups

Friendships can be pretty confusing. These resources explore
the dynamics of adolescent
social groups and may help you
figure out where you fit in and
why some kids act the way they
do. Unfortunately, there are not

a lot of resources on this subject
for boys.

*Queen Bees and Wannabees:
Helping Your Daughter Survive
Cliques, Gossip, Boyfriends and
Other Realities of Adolescence*
by Rosalind Wiseman
This book explores the lives
and friendships of girls and
offers advice on how to survive
the many ups and downs. It
contains lots of advice for
parents, but may also be
interesting to you.

*You Be Me: Friendship in the
Lives of Teen Girls*
edited by Susan Musgrave
A series of essays by young
women about their experiences
with friendship.

*Real Boys: Rescuing Our Sons
from the Myth of Boyhood*
by William Pollock
This book takes an in-depth
look at boys and the way they
are socialized in today's world.
Chapter 8 explores boys and
their friendships. It is written for
adults, but it is very readable and
you may find it interesting.

Bullying

There is a powerful documen-
tary produced by the National
Film Board of Canada called
It's a Girl's World. This film

explores the issue of friendships, cliques, and social bullying among girls. To find out more about social bullying and the film, check out www.nfb.ca and search "it's a girl's world" which will link you to the film's website.

www.stopbullyingnow.hrsa.gov
An interesting website that explores the issue of bullying, why some people bully, and the impact it can have on your life.

www.bullying.org
An international award–winning Canadian website that offers information, resources, and support on the issue of bullying. Check out their e-zine, *BE the Change!*

www.cyberbullying.ca
A website produced by the creators of www.bullying.org which explores bullying that happens online through instant messaging, e-mail, cell phones, and websites.

Genetics
Your chances of having depression increase if there is a history of depression or other mood disorders in your family. To learn more about this connection check out:

Understanding Depression: What We Know and What You Can Do about It
by J. Raymond DePaulo Jr.

Images of Perfection
The struggle to fit in can be made more difficult by our cultural obsession with beauty. These resources will help you to understand how images of beauty may affect you.

In Your Face: The Culture of Beauty and You
by Shari Graydon
A very thorough and interesting review of the history of beauty and how the culture of beauty affects our lives.

The Beauty Myth: How Images of Beauty Are Used against Women
by Naomi Wolf
An important documentation of the pressures women face in society to conform to beauty norms.

Media Literacy
Here are some particularly interesting resources that explore the impact of media on your life and new ways to look at media:

Made You Look: How Advertising Works and Why You Should Know
by Shari Graydon
Geared to teens, this book

explores how advertising works and how it can affect your life.

www.mediawatch.ca
The website of MediaWatch, a Canadian national media awareness and advocacy organization. It's got lots of interesting information on how media affect us, different ways to understand the media, and things you can do to lessen the impact of media on your life.

www.justthink.org
The website of Just Think, an organization that teaches youth to understand the words and images in the media and encourages them to think for themselves.

www.medialit.org
The website of the Center for Media Literacy, which promotes media literacy, especially in youth.

CHAPTER THREE
Depression: What Is It, Really?

Definition of Depression
There are a lot of resources that describe what adolescent depression is and how it is different from adolescent moodiness. In these same resources you will also find information about your

risk factors for depression, symptoms of depression, and ways to deal with it.

More than Moody: Recognizing and Treating Adolescent Depression
by Harold S. Koplewicz
This book is written for adults but has some very clear explanations of what depression is, and also tells the stories and experiences of youth who have struggled with depression and other mood disorders.

"Help Me, I'm Sad": Recognizing, Treating, and Preventing Childhood and Adolescent Depression by David Fassler and Lynne S. Dumas
This book contains lots of useful information on adolescent depression. Although it's written for adults, you may find it helpful.

Ups and Downs: How to Beat the Blues and Teen Depression
by Susan Klebanoff and Ellen Luborsky
A very practical and youth-friendly book that offers some good suggestions as to ways you can tackle your depression or blues.

Conquering the Beast Within: How I Fought Depression and

Won ... And How You Can, Too
by Cait Irwin
A really honest look at one
young woman's battle with
depression. She illustrated and
wrote it herself, and offers
insight and hope to anyone
struggling with depression.

*The Other Side of Blue: The Truth
about Teenage Depression*
by Elyse Dubo and Boja Vasic
in collaboration with Linda
Conn and Marshall Korenblum
An interesting video that
explores the issue of depression
through the experiences of four
teenagers. Available in Canada
from Canadian Learning
Company (800) 267-2877 and
in the U.S. from Fanlight
Productions (800) 937-4113.
May also be available through
your local library.

www.kidshealth.org/teen/your_
mind
A very youth-friendly site that
offers medical information and
advice to teens on all kinds of
mental health issues.

www.nmha.org
The website of the National
Mental Health Association.
Check out the fact sheets that
describe depression, its symp-
toms, and how to get help.

www.nimh.nih.gov
The website of the National
Institute of Mental Health
and the National Institutes of
Health. Check out the health
information section, which
explains depression, its symptoms, and how to get help.

www.mentalhealth.org
The website of the National
Mental Health Information
Center, sponsored by the United
States Department of Health
and Human Services and the
Substance Abuse and Mental
Health Services Administration.
It contains clear and helpful
information on mood disorders
in its online publications (search
"mood disorders").

Seasonal Affective Disorder

www.nmha.org
The National Mental Health
Association has an interesting
fact sheet on SAD.

www.sada.org.uk
The website of the SAD
Association, which has information on the symptoms and treatment options for SAD.

CHAPTER FOUR
Anxiety: Panic and Fear

Anxiety Disorders
Here are some resources that explain what anxiety disorders are and how they differ from everyday anxiety. They will also help you to better understand panic attacks and phobias.

Don't Panic: Taking Control of Anxiety Attacks
by R. Reid Wilson
This book explains anxiety and panic attacks and offers help to people suffering from them. It's written for adults but is easily accessible to youth.

www.adaa.org
The website of the Anxiety Disorders Association of America, containing lots of information on anxiety disorders and related issues.

www.nimh.nih.gov
The website of the National Institute of Mental Health and the National Institutes of Health. Check out the health information section, which explains anxiety disorders, symptoms, and how to get help.

www.kidshealth.org/kid/health_ problems/learning_problem/ afraid.html
This site has clear and youth-friendly information about anxiety and anxiety disorders.

www.ocfoundation.org
This is the website of the Obsessive Compulsive Foundation and focuses on the illness, symptoms, and treatments.

CHAPTER FIVE
Bipolar Disorder: Highs and Lows

Bipolar Disorder
Bipolar disorder can be a confusing and frustrating illness. Here are some resources that can help you to better understand the disorder and how you can manage it.

The Bipolar Child: The Definitive and Reassuring Guide to Childhood's Most Misunderstood Disorder by Demitri Papolos and Janice Papolos
The "big book" on bipolar disorder in children. It is written for parents but has a lot of good information on the disorder that you may find helpful.

An Unquiet Mind: A Memoir of Moods and Madness
by Kay Redfield Jamison
A beautifully written book by a psychiatrist who struggled with bipolar disorder. She tells her story with humor and sensitivity.

www.nmha.org
The website of the National
Mental Health Association.
Check out the fact sheet on
bipolar disorder.

www.dbsalliance.org
The website of the Depression
and Bipolar Support Alliance.
It has lots of information on
bipolar disorder, its treatments
and symptoms, and how to help
a friend with the disorder.

CHAPTER SIX
*Food Issues: Eating Disorders and
Disordered Eating*

Purchasing Power
These resources will explain
your influence on your family's
shopping habits and how companies market directly to you.

*Made You Look: How Advertising
Works and Why You Should Know*
by Shari Graydon
Geared to teens, this book
explores how advertising works
and how it can affect your life. It
takes a peek at how companies
market their products to kids
because they know how much
kids influence what their parents
buy.

*Wise Up to Teens: Insights into
Marketing and Advertising to*

Teenagers by Peter Zollo
This book is actually written for
corporations and marketing
companies, but it has some
interesting facts and information
on the power of the teenage
consumer.

Anorexia, Bulimia, and Binge Eating Disorder
The following resources will
explain what these conditions
are, why they happen, what the
symptoms are, how they can
affect you both physically and
emotionally, and how to get
help.

*Anorexia Nervosa: A Survival
Guide for Families, Friends and
Sufferers* by Janet Treasure
Explains anorexia nervosa and
offers support for families as
well as those suffering from the
illness.

*The Parent's Guide to Childhood
Eating Disorders* by Marcia
Herrin and Nancy Matsumoto
Contains a good overview of
eating disorders, how to identify
them, and ways to get help. It is
written for parents but has lots
of information you may find
helpful.

www.sheenasplace.org
The website of Sheena's Place,
a Toronto-based organization

supporting people suffering from eating disorders and their families. Check out their online zine, *Flushed.*

www.hedc.org
The website of the Harvard Eating Disorders Center, it contains lots of information on eating disorders, their signs and symptoms, and treatment options.

www.edap.org
The website of the National Eating Disorders Association, it has lots of information on eating disorders, their signs and symptoms, and treatment options.

www.nedic.ca
The website of the National Eating Disorder Information Centre, a Canadian organization that provides information on eating disorders. Check out the links and their recommended reading list.

CHAPTER SEVEN
Self-Mutilation: Releasing the Pain

Understanding Self-Mutilation
The issue of self-mutilation is very sensitive and often frightening. There are some interest-

ing resources that explore and explain this issue. Please be aware that some of these resources can be upsetting for people who cut or self-mutilate in other ways. As stated earlier in this book, reading about other people's experiences can be really helpful, but it can also bring back lots of memories of your own experiences, good and bad. It's important to be sure that you have the supports you need around you so that if these resources upset you or make you want to hurt yourself, you have someone to talk to.

A Bright Red Scream: Self-Mutilation and the Language of Pain by Marilee Strong
This book is intense, as it is based on interviews with over 50 people who have engaged in self-harming behavior. It tells their stories and also explores social and historical issues surrounding self-mutilation.

Cutting: Understanding and Overcoming Self-Mutilation by Stephen Levenkron
This book is full of information on self-mutilation, social issues that contribute to it, and ways to move forward. It also contains stories of people's personal experiences with self-mutilation.

www.safeincanada.ca
The website of Self-Abuse Finally Ends in Canada. This website offers hope, help, and support to people who self-injure.

CHAPTER EIGHT
Depression and Gender: The Differences between Boys and Girls

Differences between Boys and Girls
There are many obvious differences between boys and girls, but these resources explain how these differences play a role in adolescent depression.

Reviving Ophelia: Saving the Selves of Adolescent Girls
by Mary Pipher
This book is all about being an adolescent girl. It contains some interesting information on depression and the societal issues that affect it.

Raising Cain: Protecting the Emotional Life of Boys
by Dan Kindlon and Michael Thompson
Written by two child psychologists whose practices focus on boys, this book presents interesting information on the lives of boys and how depression can impact them.

Substance Use
www.freevibe.com
The website of the National Youth Anti-Drug Media Campaign. It's very youth-friendly and has lots of information on why you shouldn't use drugs and alcohol, fun downloads, and links.

Violence
www.safeyouth.org
The website of the National Youth Violence Prevention Resource Center, offering lots of information and supports on the issue of youth violence.

CHAPTER NINE
Suicide: No Turning Back

Risk Factors, Signs, and Support
Here are some great resources on suicide. They can help you identify the signs that someone you know may be thinking about suicide, and suggest what to do in this situation. They will also offer support to you if you are feeling suicidal. Please remember, though, that if you are feeling suicidal, **you need to talk with someone right away**. This is not something you should deal with on your own.

When Nothing Matters Anymore: A Survival Guide for Depressed Teens by Bev Cobain
Written by Kurt Cobain's aunt, who is a nurse, this book has lots of useful and interesting information on depression and suicide.

Helping Your Teen Overcome Depression: A Guide for Parents by Miriam Kaufman
This book is written for parents but has lots of information on depression and suicide.

Night Falls Fast: Understanding Suicide by Kay Redfield Jamison
Written by a psychiatrist who has struggled with bipolar disorder, this book explores the issue of suicide and suicide prevention.

www.catscanada.org
The website of a Canadian organization called Creating Awareness of Teenage Suicide, offering education and support to people dealing with suicide.

www.hopeline.com
The website of the National Hopeline Network, a national U.S. organization that was established in memory of Kristin Brooks Rossell, a young woman who committed suicide. This site contains information and links to support for anyone dealing with or thinking about suicide.

CHAPTER TEN
Treatment Options: Medications and Therapies

The following resources explore the many issues identified in this chapter. You will find out about the different types of counselors available to you, the kinds of therapy you may want to try, the medications that may be prescribed to you, and some alternative therapies that might appeal to you. Remember to check with your doctor before trying anything new.

Before we get into resources for specific topics, the Depression and Bipolar Support Alliance website has a great page that walks you through life after diagnosis. Check it out at http://www.dbsalliance.org/bookstore/justdiag.html

Counselors
The following two books both contain good descriptions of the different kinds of counselors or therapists who may be able to help you with your depression or other mood disorder:

*When Nothing Matters Anymore:
A Survival Guide for Depressed
Teens* by Bev Cobain

*Helping Your Teen Overcome
Depression: A Guide for Parents*
by Miriam Kaufman

www.mooddisorders.on.ca
The website of the Mood
Disorders Association of
Ontario. It contains an interesting fact sheet (called "Finding a
Therapist") that suggests where
to look for a therapist and lists
questions you might ask to find
out if a therapist is the best fit
for you. It also lists Canadian
resources on where to look for a
therapist.

www.dbsalliance.org
The website of the Depression
and Bipolar Support Alliance.
It has a fact sheet (called "Find
a Mental Health Professional")
on how and where to find help
in the U.S.

Therapies
The following two resources
clearly explain the different
types of therapy you might try.
Although both resources are
Canadian, general therapy
approaches are pretty much the
same across North America.

*It Starts Here: A Guide to Mood
Disorders for Teens* by the Mood
Disorders Association of
Ontario (MDAO)

*Helping Your Teen Overcome
Depression: A Guide for Parents*
by Dr. Miriam Kaufman

www.mentalhealth.org
The website of the National
Mental Health Information
Center, sponsored by the United
States Department of Health
and Human Services and the
Substance Abuse and Mental
Health Services Administration.
It contains clear and helpful
information on therapy options
in an online publication called
"Mental Treatment and Therapy
Guide."

Medications
There are a lot of resources that
will explain the different types
of medication that may be
prescribed to you. Your doctor
should also be able to answer
any questions that you have.

The following three books all
contain information on medications, their uses and side effects:

*It Starts Here: A Guide to Mood
Disorders for Teens* by the Mood
Disorders Association of
Ontario (MDAO)

More Than Moody: Recognizing and Treating Adolescent Depression by Harold S. Koplewicz

The Bipolar Child: The Definitive and Reassuring Guide to Childhood's Most Misunderstood Disorder by Demitri Papolos and Janice Papolos

Alternative Therapies
Alternative therapies, such as herbal medicines, relaxation, exercise, vitamin therapy, and homeopathy, are explored in the following resources. Remember to check with your doctor before trying any alternative therapies.

Helping Your Teen Overcome Depression: A Guide for Parents by Dr. Miriam Kaufman
Contains a chapter on alternative therapies available to treat adolescent depression.

When Nothing Matters Anymore: A Survival Guide for Depressed Teens by Bev Cobain
Includes information and suggestions on alternative therapies throughout the text.

www.homeopathic.org
The website of the National Center for Homeopathy, an organization that supports and promotes homeopathy in the United States. It offers information about homeopathy and its uses to treat a variety of ailments.

NOTES

Chapter 1

- history of depression: Stanley W. Jackson, *Melancholia and Depression from Hippocratic Times to Modern Times* (New Haven: Yale University Press, 1986); Andrew Solomon, *The Noonday Demon* (New York: Touchstone Books, 2001).
- Socrates quote: as cited in Peter Zollo, *Wise Up to Teens: Insights into Marketing and Advertising to Teenagers* (New York: New Strategists Publications, 1999), xiii.
- Edgar Friedenberg, *The Vanishing Adolescent* (New York: Dell, 1959), 29.
- T.S. Eliot quote: as cited on TV-Turnoff Network (http://www.tvturnoff.org/quotes.htm)
- adults as depressed adolescents: David G. Fassler and Lynne S. Dumas, *"Help Me, I'm Sad": Recognizing, Treating, and Preventing Childhood and Adolescent Depression* (New York: Viking, 1997), 4.
- acknowledgment of adolescents suffering from depression: Ibid., 11.
- number of children and teenagers in the U.S. who suffer from depression: Harold Koplewicz, *More Than Moody* (New York: G.P. Putnam's Sons, 2002), 4.
- Ibid., 5.
- factors affecting rise in adolescent depression: Fassler and Dumas, *"Help Me, I'm Sad"*, 3.
- brain development: Claudia Wallis, "What Makes Teens Tick," *Time*, Canadian Edition, May 10, 2004, 44; Koplewicz, *More Than Moody*, 35.
- brain development: Wallis, "What Makes Teens Tick," 46–47.
- abnormalities in pruning process: Ibid., 49.
- adolescent antidepressant use in the U.S.: Paul Raeburn, "The Pill Paradox," *Psychology Today*, October 2004, 75.
- overmedication of adolescents: Jeffrey Kluger, "Medicating Young Minds," *Time*, Canadian Edition, January 19, 2004, 43.
- effects of long-term medication use: Ibid., 42.
- Canadian study on ineffectiveness of antidepressants in adolescents: "Anti-depressants Found Ineffective on Teenagers," *The Globe and Mail*, February 17, 2004.
- use of antidepressants may increase risk of suicide: Jonathan Mahler, "The Antidepressant Dilemma," *The New York Times Magazine*, November 21, 2004, 59.
- combination therapy as most effective: "Anti-depressants Found Ineffective on Teenagers," *The Globe and Mail*, February 17, 2004.
- black box warning: U.S. Food & Drug Administration (http://www.fda.gov/cder/drug/antidepressants/SSRIPHA200410.htm)
- celebrities, creativity, and mood disorders: Mood Disorders Association of Ontario, *It Starts Here: A Guide to Mood Disorders for Teens* (Toronto, 2002), 58; Kay Redfield Jamison, *Touched with Fire: Manic-Depressive*

Illness and the Artistic Temperament (New York: Free Press Paperbacks, 1993); "Celebrity Meltdown," *Psychology Today*, November/December 1999.

Chapter 2
- Edgar Friedenberg, *The Vanishing Adolescent* (New York: Dell, 1959), 37.
- sex hormones affecting pruning process in brain: Claudia Wallis, "What Makes Teens Tick," *Time*, Canadian Edition, May 10, 2004, 47.
- stress may alter brain chemistry: Harold Koplewicz, *More Than Moody* (New York: G.P. Putnam's Sons, 2002), 36–37.
- the function of serotonin in the brain: Andrew Solomon, *The Noonday Demon* (New York: Touchstone Books, 2001), 112.
- resiliency: Miriam Kaufman, *Helping Your Teen Overcome Depression* (Toronto: Key Porter Books, 2000), 245; David G. Fassler and Lynne S. Dumas, *"Help Me, I'm Sad": Recognizing, Treating, and Preventing Childhood and Adolescent Depression* (New York: Viking, 1997), 172.
- poverty and depression: Solomon, *The Noonday Demon*, 336.
- genetics and depression: Koplewicz, *More Than Moody*, 83; J. Raymond DePaulo Jr., *Understanding Depression* (Hoboken, NJ: John Wiley & Sons, 2002), 88.
- violence in the media: United States Department of Health & Human Services, Office of the Surgeon General, *Youth Violence: A Report of the Surgeon General* (January 2001) (http://www.surgeongeneral.gov/library/youthviolence/)
- sexual content in the media: RAND Corporation, *Does Watching Sex on Television Influence Teens' Sexual Activity?* (http://www.rand.org/ publications /RB/RB9068/RB9068.pdf)

Chapter 3
- reactive depression: Harold Koplewicz, *More Than Moody* (New York: G.P. Putnam's Sons, 2002), 15.
- clinical depression and rates of: Ibid.
- cohort effect: D. and J. Papolos, *The Bipolar Child* (New York: Broadway Books, 2002), 163.
- adolescent girls and depression: David G. Fassler and Lynne S. Dumas, *"Help Me, I'm Sad": Recognizing, Treating, and Preventing Childhood and Adolescent Depression* (New York: Viking, 1997), 17.
- signs and symptoms of depression: Bev Cobain, *When Nothing Matters Anymore: A Survival Guide for Depressed Teens* (Minneapolis: Free Spirit Publishing, 1998), 13–18, 25–26.
- differences between depressed adults and adolescents: Koplewicz, *More Than Moody*, 16–17.
- the four major types of depression: Ibid., 14–15.
- melatonin and SAD: National Mental Health Association (http://www.nmha.org/infoctr/factsheets/27.cfm); Andrew Solomon, *The Noonday Demon* (New York: Touchstone Books, 2001), 140.

Chapter 4
- anxiety and depression: J. Raymond DePaulo Jr., *Understanding Depression* (Hoboken, NJ: John Wiley & Sons, 2002), 16.
- clinical depression and anxiety disorders: Harold Koplewicz, *More Than Moody* (New York: G.P. Putnam's Sons, 2002), 51.
- similar nerve and brain pathways in depression and anxiety disorders: DePaulo, *Understanding Depression*, 17.
- five major types of anxiety disorder: National Institute of Mental Health (http://www.nimh.nih.gov/); National Mental Health Association (http://www.nmha.org/)
- symptoms of panic attack: Miriam Kaufman, *Helping Your Teen Overcome Depression* (Toronto: Key Porter Books, 2000), 141–42.
- panic attacks: National Mental Health Association (http://www.nmha.org/infoctr/factsheets/32.cfm)
- U.S. statistics on panic disorder: Ibid.
- caffeine and panic attacks: National Alliance for the Mentally Ill (http://www.nami.org/Content/ContentGroups/Helpline1/Panic_Disorder_.htm)
- drug use and depression and anxiety: Koplewicz, *More Than Moody*, 206.
- specific phobias: About.com (http://www.psychology.about.com/library/bl/blglos.phobias.htm)

Chapter 5
- rates of bipolar disorder in the U.S.: Depression and Bipolar Support Alliance (http://www.dbsalliance.org/info/bipolar.html)
- symptoms of bipolar disorder mistaken for other childhood disorders: D. and J. Papolos, *The Bipolar Child* (New York: Broadway Books, 2002), 5.
- symptoms of mania: Depression and Bipolar Support Alliance (http://www.dbsalliance.org/info/bipolar.html)
- symptoms of depression: Ibid.
- statistics on bipolar disorder: Jeffrey Kluger, "Young and Bipolar," *Time*, Canadian Edition, August 19, 2002, 35.
- estimated rates of depressed children who will develop bipolar disorder: Papolos, *The Bipolar Child*, 4.
- use of antidepressants can cause mania in someone who is bipolar: Ibid., xvi.
- types of bipolar disorder: Kluger, "Young and Bipolar."
- other characteristics of bipolar disorder: Papolos, *The Bipolar Child*, 16.
- facts on bipolar disorder: Kluger, "Young and Bipolar."

Chapter 6
- influence of adolescents over parents' purchasing decisions: Shari Graydon, *Made You Look: How Advertising Works and Why You Should Know* (Toronto: Annick Press, 2003), 18.
- disordered eating vs. eating disorders: adapted from the Harvard Eating

Disorders Center website (www.hedc.org)
- risk of developing an eating disorder: M. Herrin and N. Matsumoto, *The Parent's Guide to Childhood Eating Disorders* (NewYork: Henry Holt, 2002), 126.
- foods that can affect your mood: Andrew Solomon, *The Noonday Demon* (New York: Touchstone Books, 2001), 138.
- an eating disorder is not a diet ...: Harvard Eating Disorders Center (www.hedc.org)
- eating disorders have the highest mortality rate ...: Sheena's Place (http://www.sheenasplace.org/quickfacts/facts.html)
- anorexia nervosa: Sheena's Place (http://www.sheenasplace.org/quickfacts/anornerv.html)
- bulimia nervosa: Sheena's Place (http://www.sheenasplace.org/quickfacts/bulinerv.html)
- binge eating disorder: Sheena's Place (http://www.sheenasplace.org/quickfacts/bingeeating.html)
- genetics and eating disorders: J. Treasure, *Anorexia Nervosa: A Survival Guide for Families, Friends and Sufferers* (East Sussex, U.K.: Psychology Press, 2000), 15; Herrin and Matsumoto, *The Parent's Guide to Childhood Eating Disorders*, 126.
- boys and eating disorders: Harvard Eating Disorders Center (www.hedc.org)
- Forty percent of fourth-graders diet ...: Ibid.
- physical effects of eating disorders: National Eating Disorders Association (http://www.edap.org/p.asp?WebPage_ID=286&Profile_ID=41143)
- Fifteen percent of people who develop anorexia ...: Sheena's Place (http://www.sheenasplace.org/quickfacts/anornerv.html)
- antidepressants as treatment for eating disorders: Herrin and Matsumoto, *The Parent's Guide to Childhood Eating Disorders*, 264.
- physical consequences of weight loss: Sheena's Place (http://www.sheenasplace.org/quickfacts/anornerv.html)
- physical consequences of bulimia: Sheena's Place (http://www.sheenasplace.org/quickfacts/bulinerv.html)
- behaviors associated with anorexia: Sheena's Place (http://www.sheenasplace.org/quickfacts/anornerv.html)
- behaviors associated with bulimia: Sheena's Place (http://www.sheenasplace.org/quickfacts/bulinerv.html)

Chapter 7
- Mary Pipher, *Reviving Ophelia* (New York: Ballantine Books, 1994), 158.
- The title of Marilee Strong's book, *A Bright Red Scream: Self-Mutilation and the Language of Pain*, resonates.
- dissociative state: Steven Levenkron, *Cutting: Understanding and*

Overcoming Self-Mutilation (New York: W.W. Norton, 1998), 109.
• self-mutilation as an addiction: Marilee Strong, *A Bright Red Scream: Self-Mutilation and the Language of Pain* (New York: Penguin Books, 1998), 106.
• history of body modification: Ibid., 140.
• agitation of bipolar disorder: D. and J. Papolos, *The Bipolar Child* (New York: Broadway Books, 2002), 44.
• sexual abuse and self-mutilation: Strong, *A Bright Red Scream*, 93.
• eating disorders and self-mutilation: Ibid., 116.

Chapter 8
• rates of depression in girls: David G. Fassler and Lynne S. Dumas, *"Help Me, I'm Sad": Recognizing, Treating, and Preventing Childhood and Adolescent Depression* (New York: Viking, 1997), 17.
• depression in boys: Ibid., 18.
• boys' behavior can mask depression: Dan Kindlon and Michael Thompson, *Raising Cain: Protecting the Emotional Life of Boys* (New York: Ballantine Books, 1999), 159.
• girls internalizing anger: Harold Koplewicz, *More Than Moody* (New York: G.P. Putnam's Sons, 2002), 80.
• rates of depression in girls after puberty: Ibid., 80; Bev Cobain, *When Nothing Matters Anymore: A Survival Guide for Depressed Teens* (Minneapolis: Free Spirit Publishing, 1998), 25.
• early puberty and onset of depression in girls: Koplewicz, *More Than Moody*, 81; J. Raymond DePaulo Jr., *Understanding Depression* (Hoboken, NJ: John Wiley & Sons, 2002), 143.
• women synthesize serotonin slower than men: Andrew Solomon, *The Noonday Demon* (New York: Touchstone Books, 2001), 174.
• social factors that influence rates of depression in girls: Koplewicz, *More Than Moody*, 81.
• social factors affecting boys: Kindlon and Thompson, *Raising Cain*, 159.
• substance use and depression: Koplewicz, *More Than Moody*, 57.
• substance use as self-destructive behavior: Fassler and Dumas, *"Help Me, I'm Sad"*, 110.
• drug use and boys: Kindlon and Thompson, *Raising Cain*, 177.
• high-risk behavior related to drug and alcohol use in boys: Ibid., 183.
• expectations of masculinity in boys can mask depression: Ibid., 158–59.
• rise in girl violence: National Youth Violence Prevention Resource Center (www.safeyouth.org); Julie Scelfo, "Bad Girls Go Wild," *Newsweek*, June 13, 2005 (http://www.msnbc.msn.com/id/8101517/site/newsweek/).
• social factors in suicide: Koplewicz, *More Than Moody*, 243–44.

Chapter 9
• reasons for increase in suicide and depression: David G. Fassler and Lynne S. Dumas, *"Help Me, I'm Sad": Recognizing, Treating, and Preventing*

Childhood and Adolescent Depression (New York: Viking, 1997), 2–4.
• statistics on suicide in the U.S.: National Center for Injury Prevention and
Control (http://www.cdc.gov/ncipc/factsheets/suifacts.htm)
• statistics on teen suicide in the U.S.: American Foundation for Suicide
Prevention (http://www.afsp.org/index-1.htm)
• risk factors for suicide: Fassler and Dumas, *"Help Me, I'm Sad"*, 103–8.
• triggers for suicide: Harold Koplewicz, *More Than Moody* (New York: G.P.
Putnam's Sons, 2002), 244–45.
• signs to look out for: Bev Cobain, *When Nothing Matters Anymore:
A Survival Guide for Depressed Teens* (Minneapolis: Free Spirit Publishing,
1998), 94–95.
• what you can do: Ibid., 95–97.

Chapter 10
• types of counselors: Miriam Kaufman, *Helping Your Teen Overcome
Depression* (Toronto: Key Porter Books, 2000), 79–82; Bev Cobain, *When
Nothing Matters Anymore: A Survival Guide for Depressed Teens*
(Minneapolis: Free Spirit Publishing, 1998), 110–11.
• types of therapy: Mood Disorders Association of Ontario, *It Starts Here:
A Guide to Mood Disorders for Teens* (Toronto, 2004), 22–25; J. Raymond
DePaulo Jr., *Understanding Depression* (Hoboken, NJ: John Wiley & Sons,
2002), 196–202.
• side effects of SSRIs: Harold Koplewicz, *More Than Moody* (New York:
G.P. Putnam's Sons, 2002), 270; Kaufman, *Helping Your Teen*, 62.
• SSRIs, MAOIs, and atypical antidepressants: Koplewicz, *More Than
Moody*, 265–74.
• medications to treat bipolar disorder: D. and J. Papolos, *The Bipolar Child*
(New York: Broadway Books, 2002), 78.
• side effects of lithium: Ibid., 82.
• drug interactions with Depakote and Tegretol: Ibid., 89–92 (includes a
complete list).
• abruptly stopping lithium increases risk of suicide: Ibid., 85.
• effects of stopping antidepressants abruptly: Kaufman, *Helping Your Teen*,
61.
• early treatment and increased risk for suicide: Ibid., 62; Andrew Solomon,
The Noonday Demon (New York: Touchstone Books, 2001), 80.
• herbal remedies: DePaulo, *Understanding Depression*, 220–28; Mood
Disorders Association of Ontario, *It Starts Here*, 26.
• alternative therapies: Kaufman, *Helping Your Teen*, 97–113.

INDEX

Index